FOUR PERIODS

IN THE

LIFE OF THE CHURCH

BY

HENRY FERGUSON, M. A.

Northam Professor of History and Political Science in Trinity College, Hartford.

NEW YORK

JAMES POTT & COMPANY

114 FIFTH AVENUE

1894

PREFACE.

The following lectures were delivered in Christ Church, Hartford, Conn., in the Lent of 1892, and have been printed at the suggestion of some of those who heard them at that time, and thought them useful. They are now presented to a larger audience, with some diffidence, but with the hope that they may accomplish at least their original object of directing the attention of those who read them to the wonderful treasury of interest and instruction which we possess in the history of the Church of Christ. It has seemed advisable to preserve the form in which they were delivered, as the lectures make no pretence to that thoroughness of treatment which would enable them to claim the title of historical essays, but are simply an attempt to give in a brief space

a general view of ecclesiastical history. No
one can expect or desire originality in an
historical lecture ; truth, not novelty, must
be the aim of the speaker ; yet every one has
a slightly different manner of regarding old
truths, and it is hoped that old friends will
not be found to suffer from a new presenta-
tion.

The main thought underlying the lectures,
the only characteristic feature of the treatment of the subject, is that the Christian
Church is an organism, and that conse-
quently, its progress has been conditioned by
the laws of organic life. It is the hope of the
author, that what he has written may be of
use to emphasize the truth, which is perhaps
the most important of all the many important
truths in regard to the Church, that it is one
and the same in all its ages of existence, living
now by the same Divine Life which inspired
it at the beginning, filled with the same
Spirit, and effecting the presence of the same
Lord ; that it is the same organism to-day
as in the days of Ignatius or of Augustine,
of Hildebrand or of Luther and Cranmer :

one, in spite of its many apparent divisions ; holy, in spite of the errors and frailties of men ; catholic or universal, more truly now than ever before in all its history; apostolic, because the secret of its life, now as always, lies in its obedience to its original apostolic commission : " Go ye into all the world, and preach the Gospel to every creature."

It has seemed inadvisable to add any notes or references, as the statements can easily be substantiated by any trustworthy ecclesiastical history, and experience has taught the author that it is very difficult to secure the perusal of anything in fine print.

With the earnest desire that more and more may learn the great attractiveness of Church History, these lectures are presented as a general introduction to the subject.

TRINITY COLLEGE, HARTFORD,
    SEPTEMBER, 1894.

CONTENTS.

LECTURE I.

LECTURE II.

LECTURE III.

LECTURE IV.

LECTURE I.

THE CHURCH OF THE FIRST THREE CENTURIES.

LECTURE I.

THE CHURCH OF THE FIRST THREE CENTURIES.

In the narrow limits of four lectures, I can attempt nothing more than to indicate in the merest outline some of the principal features of the life-history of that wonderful organization, in which we Christians of to-day are joined together with saints, apostles, confessors, martyrs, in one body, of which the head and the life is our Lord Jesus Christ.

To do more than this would be impossible; the Evangelist himself declares that the world would not contain the books that might be written of the doings and sayings of our Lord alone. Time would fail, indeed, to tell of the Gedeons and Baraks and Samsons of our Christian commonwealth. On the other hand, it seems equally impossible

11

to condense into such narrow limits even a summary of what are the most important events of the history of the world, or in so short a space to give a general view that can be in the least satisfactory or trustworthy. Yet, though much must be sacrificed, there may be use and benefit even in an outline, and though it is a proverb that mistakes are apt to lurk under the shadow of generalizations, yet generalizations are necessary for a complete view of any subject. It is possible to exaggerate minute knowledge of detail into error ; and when so much calls for our attention, it is desirable to dwell upon great, distinguishing, characteristic features, rather than upon those which, however valuable and interesting, are yet subordinate. For these reasons, and with this hope, I shall venture to lay before you a general sketch of four important periods in Church history.

1. The Church of the First Three Centuries.

2. The Church of the Christian Empire.

3. The Church of Western Europe.

4. The Reformation in the Sixteenth Century.

First in interest and importance, as in chronological order, is the history of the Church in the early ages of its existence, the period of its origin, of its early development, of its heroic struggle for life; persecuted, but not forsaken; cast down, but not destroyed; always bearing about in the body the dying of the Lord Jesus, and therefore manifesting in its mortal flesh the life of its immortal King. In this first period it will be convenient to make three further subdivisions. The age of the apostles naturally stands alone, distinguished by the personal authority of those whom the Lord himself had selected as his agents and ambassadors, and upon whom special gifts of the Holy Ghost were bestowed for their work of laying the foundations of the Church. This is, properly speaking, the period of *origins*, and our authority for it is contained in those books, written by the apostles themselves or their companions, which the Church has selected from all other early writings as espe-

cially authoritative.   The second subdivision
comprises the lifetime of those men who immediately followed the apostles, under whose
guidance the institutions of the Church were
developed, the sacred books collected, and the
general lines of doctrine and practice established.   For this period, our authorities are
fewer in number, and we cannot refer with
as absolute confidence to them as to the books
of the New Testament ; yet materials enough
exist to enable us to form, with a tolerable
degree of certainty, a conception of its character.   This is the time of *formation* and *development*.   It may be roughly said to extend
to the middle or end of the second century of
our era.   The third subdivision is that of the
Church in conflict with the heathen world,
the period of *struggle* and persecution, ter-
minated by the final victory of the Christian
Faith in the beginning of the fourth century.
For this period our authorities are numerous,
and we have little difficulty, with their aid,
in reproducing to our minds the condition of
the Christian society in its time of severest
trial.

In each of these periods, a great advance was made, and a critical step was taken. In the first, the Church separated itself distinctly from Judaism : in the second, it separated itself distinctly from the philosophical systems of the Gentile mind ; in the third, it separated itself distinctly from the social and political life of the Roman world. In each period there was a struggle and a progressive movement : a struggle against a tendency that threatened to cripple and restrict the Church, a progress towards a position of greater freedom and dignity. In the apostolic age it was clearly shown that the Church was not to be one of the divisions of Judaism, but the successor of them all; in the sub-apostolic, that it was not to be one of the many schools of religious philosophy, but a true religion ; in the third, that it was not to be one of the many religions of the Roman world, but the one only faith, the only truth, the only religion.

I.

THE history of the Church begins with the day of Pentecost. Our Lord had founded his kingdom, had chosen his apostles, and had given them their commission while he was still with them, but had bidden them tarry in Jerusalem until they should be endued with power from on high to undertake the work for which he had selected them. When the appointed day arrived, the promised Spirit was sent upon them, and the work of the Church as an active body at once began ; Christian doctrine was proclaimed ; converts were received into union with the new society by the sacrament of baptism, and the organization at once adopted a distinct manner of life. What this was, is summed up for us in St. Luke's short impressive sentences : "They continued stedfastly in the apostles' doctrine and fellowship, and in breaking of bread, and in prayers. And fear came upon every soul : and many wonders and signs were done by the Apostles. And all that believed were together, and had all things common ; and sold their posses- sions and goods, and parted them to all men, as every man had need."

The early persecutions, by the Sadducee rulers of the Jews, had only the effect of add- ing daily to the disciples multitudes both of men and women, a great company even of the priests becoming obedient to the faith, and of giving to the infant movement the support of popular sympathy, especially among the party of the Pharisees. The rapidly increasing number of the converts, most of whom were from the poorer classes, led to the necessity of organization in the system of distributing the supplies of the little community. "There arose a murmur- ing of the Grecians against the Hebrews, be- cause their widows were neglected in the daily ministration." These murmurs were the occasion of the first step that is recorded towards the formation of a regular ministry, the appointment of the seven, to relieve the apostles in the work of ministering to the

2

temporal necessities of the faithful, and to free them for their more especial duty of preaching the word of God.

These seven were chosen from the Hellenists, or Greek speaking Jews, men of the dispersion, who had been attracted to Jerusalem by the Temple services and festivals. They were men of devotion and of earnestness, "full of the Holy Ghost and of faith," natural leaders of their fellows, and we find them, at once, active in the defence and promulgation of the faith, as well as in their more secular duties. The preaching of Stephen produced the first severe persecution, arousing against the Christians the hostility of the Pharisaic party, which till then had been friendly towards them ; and the persecution had the effect of scattering the living fire of Christianity outside the limits of Jerusalem.

Steadily we hear of the enlargement and expansion of the Church. First, the Samaritans, hated and despised by the strict Jews as schismatics, were brought to the faith by the preaching of Philip, who, like Stephen,

was one of the seven ; then came the conversion and baptism of the Ethiopian eunuch,
probably a proselyte to the Jewish faith, also
a work of the same spiritual enthusiasm
which had carried the gospel to Samaria ;
then the baptism of Cornelius the Roman
centurion, a proselyte indeed, but still an
uncircumcised Gentile ; and finally, at Antioch, the heathen themselves were brought
to the light of life. The most bitter of all
the persecutors of the infant Church became
one of its most earnest adherents ; the Phar-
isee Saul, who had held the garments of
those who had stoned Stephen, and had
breathed out threatenings and slaughter
against the disciples of the Lord, became
Paul the apostle, the special messenger of
Christ to the Gentiles.

The great change of conception which was
involved in the admission of the Gentiles into
the Christian fellowship did not come without strong and bitter opposition. There was
a powerful party among the Christians at
Jerusalem that was made up of converts
from the Pharisees. These were ready to

accept Jesus as the Messiah, and believed in
his resurrection and in his coming again,
but do not seem to have considered him
divine, or to have appreciated that his message was for all mankind. Their mental
horizon was limited by the borders of Palestine and the requirements of the Mosaic law ;
if Gentiles wished to share the blessings
which the Son of David had brought to his
people, they must make themselves his
people by submitting to that people's law.
They had endured the admission of the Samaritans and the Ethiopian to fellowship
with them, and had yielded to the divine in-
timation which had guided the dealings of St.
Peter with Cornelius, but the proceedings of
the missionaries at Antioch seemed to them
utterly without justification. In spite of the
favorable reports from the messengers whom
the apostles had sent to inquire into the
matter, they were shocked and alarmed at
what was done ; and, acting independently of
their leaders in the Church, they sent down
their emissaries, who stirred up bitterness
and confusion in the little congregation of

Gentile Christians in Antioch, and in those which had been established by Paul and Barnabas in the adjacent lands. The question was appealed promptly to the apostles and elders at Jerusalem, and there settled by a wise compromise ; yet, for a long time, this spirit of opposition to St. Paul and his work survived, and vexed the peace of the Church, until, after the awful tragedy of the destruction of Jerusalem, the few who remained unconvinced separated from their brethren, and became the founders of one of the first heretical sects, the Ebionites.

The importance of the step that was taken at Antioch, and ratified by the apostles at Jerusalem, can hardly be over-estimated. The Church shook off the grave-clothes with which the lovers of a dead past would have bound it, and rose to a full consciousness of its high mission—to preach to all the world the unsearchable riches of Christ. Had the opposite counsels prevailed, had the apostles been untrue to their commission, unfaithful to the Spirit within them, Christianity must have sunk to the level of the Jewish sects about it, and have perished in the destruction of Jerusalem. The Lord's promise had been that the gates of hell should not prevail against his Church. This was the first great victory, in fulfilment of his word. The Church henceforward separated itself definitely from the synagogue. It was not to be narrowed, but to broaden and extend, until like the mustard seed of the parable it should "shoot out great branches, so that the fowls of the air should lodge under the shadow of it."

Of the history of the first Christian missions we have only the few typical instances recorded in the Acts of the Apostles ; of the way in which the Church was elsewhere planted and extended, little is known. The early missionaries were workers rather than writers of history, content, as long as the work was done, that their part in it should remain unrecorded. We do not even know what, or where, were the labors of the apostles themselves. Christian tradition has preserved the memory of the resting-places of but four of them ; and of their work, besides what is recorded in the Acts, we have only the slightest fragments of information overgrown with legendary embellishment. But however it was that the work was done, the gospel was preached during their lifetime in all the principal places of the Roman world, and churches were formed in such a way as to show agreement among their founders in doctrine, organization, and practice.

The early organization of the Church was simple, but contained in the germ all those features which in the next generation, when the personal leadership of the apostles was removed, were developed into a definite and uniform system of church government. The Church did not spring into existence with its organization ready made, but, upon principles laid down in the lifetime of the apostles, which it is not incredible may have been suggested by our Lord himself, it formed for itself, under the guidance of the Spirit, a practical and simple polity, so well adapted to its purpose that it has survived the storms of eighteen centuries, and testifies to-day, by

its existence and adaptiveness, to its natural,
and therefore divine, character.   Wherever
Christianity spread congregations were gathered together, those in the smaller places
grouped around larger centres ; organized,
partly after the pattern of the Jewish syna-
gogues, partly after the model of charitable
societies and guilds among the Greeks.   Side
by side, and interchangeable with each other,
we find in the New Testament the names of
elders and of bishops, one recalling the synagogue and the other the guild, and in like
manner the names of ministers and deacons.
The name apostle, which had been given by
our Lord to the twelve whom he had chosen,
is conferred upon several others besides them,
such as Matthias, Paul, and Barnabas, and,
probably also, Epaphroditus, Andronicus,
and Junia ; while, on the other hand, both
St. Peter and St. John describe themselves
by the title presbyter or elder.   In the
interchange of these names we may see a
picture of the character of the early Church.
Its heads were apostles—messengers divinely
sent and commissioned ; they were also

elders—the natural rulers of their congregations, the heirs of all that was best and truest
in Judaism; they were also overseers or
bishops—to feed the flock of God committed
to their charge, thus joining together with the
ideas of mission and of rulership the functions of the Greek ἐπίσκοποι to administer the
funds and property of the society for the
benefit of its members, and to be the friends
and protectors of the poor. Other names
appear which failed to become permanent
titles, such as prophets, evangelists, pastors,
teachers, helps.* In some churches the
apostle ruled directly ; in most, however,
this office was performed by the elder or
council of elders, who had under them
several ministers or deacons, while the
apostles gave a general oversight, besides
devoting themselves to opening new fields
of work.

* The term prophet seems to have been used in a tech-
nical sense as the name of a particular class of Christian
teachers, until it became discredited from its abuse by
the Montanists in the end of the second century.

II.

THERE is danger in breadth as well as in narrowness; in liberalism as well as in conservatism; and in the second period of the Church's history it was necessary to struggle against a temptation which came from the very victory over the cramping and belittling spirit of the Judaizing party. In becoming a Gentile religion, Christianity was exposed to the inroads of Gentile philosophy. As the danger in the first generation had been that the Church might be content to remain one of several Jewish sects, so, now, the danger was that it should become only one of the many schools of oriental or Greek speculation. Strange travesties of Christian doctrine arose, in which the mysteries of redemption were mingled with the fancies of Greek mystics, and with the wild conjectures of oriental theosophy. Every fantastic belief of the ancient world seemed to hasten to welcome the new faith as akin to it, and to endeavor to absorb it, or compel it to join in its wild phantasmagoria. Monstrous forms of belief arose, in which holy names and words were mingled with a mystic jargon which could never have been intelligible even to the initiated. This farrago of nonsense was boastfully called knowledge, *Gnosis*, and was considered to be the quintessence of speculative truth ; while the humbler Christians, who were not able to attain to its heights, were looked down upon as unworthy the attention of the illuminated. Its votaries picked and chose among the hardly formulated beliefs of the Church, rejected or accepted books to suit their own arbitrary fancies, and, had they succeeded in convincing the common sense of Christianity, would have soon explained away the faith into a most obscure and profitless philosophy. To oppose this tendency was the intellectual task of the second generation of Christians ; and they did it by opposing, to the false knowledge, a true knowledge, based upon the simple facts of the faith they had received ; to the false philosophy of its votaries, the true philosophy of St. John and St. Paul. The work was thoroughly done; and by the middle of the second century, a clear line had been drawn between profitable study of the mysteries of God and the unprofitable dreams of conceited and opinionated sophists, who were recognized as aliens and, grouped together under one convenient title, were known as Gnostic heretics. Thus, in the sub-apostolic age also, was there an advance made and a line of distinction drawn; and Christianity refused to evaporate itself into oriental fantasy, as it had refused to burden itself with the yoke of the Jewish law.

The Church was aided in its first struggle with heresy by its now completed organization and by the zeal and discrimination with which its members collected and used the writings of the previous generation. We know, it is true, but little about the history of the transition from the apostolic Church, where the authority was in the hands of the apostles, and where few, if any, of them, seem to have had special or restricted fields of work, to the organic system which succeeded it, with its threefold ministry, and its clear differentiation of functions. One system, however, succeeds the other without a break. Some traces may be found of the development even in the apostles' lifetime : James, the Lord's brother, held at Jerusalem a position closely resembling that of a later diocesan bishop ; Paul sent Timothy to Ephesus and Titus to Crete, with definite instructions as to rule and government ; and, in the Apocalypse, the Seven Churches of Asia are addressed in the persons of their angels or bishops. Clement, St. Paul's companion, the earliest of the non-canonical writers, and according to tradition bishop of Rome, states plainly that the apostles had made arrangements in regard to the proper succession of the ministry ; and Ignatius of Antioch, writing very shortly after the death of St. John, represents the episcopal system as in full vigor, and urges subordination to it, without a word to indicate that the system he recommended was new. Before the second century had elapsed, we find established in all the churches, in all parts of the world, one system, everywhere alike, whatever else might be the local differences, even the heretical sects having the same organization. Everywhere we find the bishops, acting as the successors of the apostles, ruling the Church, ordaining the presbyters, and administering, either personally, or by means of their assistants the deacons, the revenues that arose from the offerings of the faithful. Everywhere also do we find a second order of ministry, known as presbyters, whose duty it was to minister in religious things in the several congregations in the various towns; and a third order, the deacons, who were the almoners and aids of the bishops. This system was found everywhere, the few exceptions which a minute investigation with difficulty succeeds in extracting from antiquity simply proving the universality of the rule. This system was either established with the knowledge and approval of the apostles, or it was not. If it was not in accordance with their instructions, it presents the amazing phenomenon of the Church in the generation immediately following the apostles, while professing to be guided by their teaching and ruled by their example, yet casting it aside all over the world at the same time, for a new and different organization.

And as everywhere the organization was the same in these fundamental points, so everywhere was there a general agreement in doctrine and in practice. It is true that differences arose, from time to time, which developed into heresies ; but this very fact proves more clearly than anything else, that there was a standard of faith from which these doctrines differed, and by which opinions were tested and condemned. Wherever a Christian went, all the world over, he found himself at home, and among brethren of a common faith. So careful were they of this standard of faith, the precious deposit with which they were entrusted, that it was not committed to writing, but taught orally to those who were being prepared for baptism.

Christian theology had come into existence at the centres of Christian life and thought, in order to controvert the heretical gainsayers, but the Church at large was rather practical than theological. The Gospels and Epistles had been collected, and were respected everywhere, and were read in public worship together with the scriptures of the Old Testament. The great act of worship was the sacrament of the Lord's Supper, which at first was administered at the close of a simple feast of brotherly love and fellowship ; but at an early date, probably during the lifetime of the apostles, this practice proved inconvenient and inexpedient, and the Agape or love feast was separated from the sacramental meal, which was then administered as a distinctly religious act, at the early meetings of the faithful held at dawn of day.   Discipline was maintained by a system of public confession and public penance, and in serious cases, by the exclusion of the offender from the fellowship of the Church. Baptism was administered to children as well as adults, though at an early date the custom grew up of deferring the sacrament until late in life, from an exaggerated conception of the danger of post-baptismal sin.

The different churches were in frequent communication with one another, and from the very first the practice prevailed of giving commendatory letters to those who went from one church to another. The Christians lived simple lives; they had renounced the world; they looked for the speedy coming again of the Lord in judgment, and lived as in the expectation of that Day. The joys of heaven were constantly before their eyes, conceived under somewhat material imagery —as were also the pains of hell—and in both they believed most literally and fervently. By the end of the second century, the empire was filled with Christian congregations, in every place of importance, and in many remote country districts as well; and it was the proud boast of Tertullian, that tribes that had repelled the Roman legions, countries inaccessible to the Roman eagles, had been invaded and conquered by the soldiers of Christ. "Camp, forum, city, market-place, and country village," he cries, "we fill them all; we leave you your temples only!"

3

III.

As the number of believers increased, it was inevitable that they should come into conflict with the civil society in which they lived. They were in the midst of a world in which the practice of idolatry entered into every action of daily life and colored the whole habit of thought. At first, the tolerant system of the Roman state religion saw in them only either a sect of the Jews, more scrupulous and more perverse than common, or a new form of philosophy, more irrational than the others, and treated them with a careless contempt. There is no reason to believe that either Nero or Domitian persecuted the Christians as Christians. They dealt with them as more objectionable than the other Jews, and attributed to them a gloomy unsociability and a perverse superstition that inspired them with hatred of the human race. Soon, however, the increasing numbers of the Christians and the antipathy shown to them by the Jews, called them to the attention of the Roman officials in the provinces, especially in Asia Minor. The temples were deserted, they complained, the sacrifices neglected, and this new sect was beginning to enter into conflict with the time-honored customs of the empire. The Roman law was very severe in regard to unlicensed organizations, and it was as such that the Christian communities were considered. There is a most interesting correspondence preserved, between the younger Pliny, who was governor of Bithynia, and the Emperor Trajan, which gives us a picture of the life of the Church in the beginning of the second century. Pliny writes, that he found on investigation that the Christians met together before daybreak, and sang hymns to Christ as God, and then bound themselves by a sacramental oath to do no wrong. Neither torture nor any other compulsion could extort any confession of wrong-doing, and he writes in perplexity to the Emperor to know how such cases were to be treated. The policy suggested by

Trajan was that which was generally followed for more than a hundred years : if the Christians were quiet, they were not to be molested nor their organization investigated; but if complaint was made and they persisted in their obstinacy, they were to be punished. Their offence was in presuming to differ from the practice of the world, in condemning the life of the world about them, and in organizing themselves into a secret society.*

---

*Some recent writers, notably Professor Ramsay, in his most scholarly and scientific " Church in the Roman Empire," are inclined to maintain that, from almost the first, the Empire was hostile to the rising Christian body, as such. They therefore hold that, in the rescript of Trajan, we have, not the first official statement of imperial policy, but what was in reality a relaxation of the severity which had prevailed under previous law. Mr. Ramsay maintains this view with great learning and ingenuity, but seems to rate less highly than it deserves, the testimony of Tertullian, who, though somewhat later, is a well-informed and capable witness. Now, Tertullian certainly did not consider that the policy enunciated by Trajan was any relaxation of the law, or anything of the nature of a *modus vivendi*, but is very severe in his condemnation of the Emperor, for what he considers illogical and inequitable conclusions.

But as time went on the differences between them and their neighbors became more strongly marked, and the popular antipathy to the unsocial Christians, who hated as was supposed all the rest of mankind, increased apace and became a source of danger even greater than the penalties of the law. Did the Nile refuse to rise high enough to fertilize the plains of Egypt, or did the Tiber rise too high and flood the low-lying quarters of the city, the cry of the mob was the same— " The Christians are to blame ! the Christians to the lions ! " Popularity-seeking governors would gratify their people by dragging to the altars the hated Christians, and offering them the alternative of sacrifice or death. In the reign of the philosophic Marcus Aurelius, the best of all the Emperors, Polycarp, A. D. the aged bishop of Smyrna, was 161–180. brought to the stake and there " played the man " before the proconsul of Asia. The same reign saw the awful sufferings of the martyrs at Vienne in Gaul, who died deaths of fearful torment rather than deny their

Lord. But down to the time of the Em-
A. D. peror Decius, in the third century,
249–251. there was no general persecution, in
which the Roman imperial power as such was
directed against the Church as such. Christians indeed were often persecuted, and were
often called upon to testify to their Master by
a martyr's death, but the danger was rather
from the people among whom they lived, than
from the rulers of the land.

It was not an easy thing to be a Christian
then, even though general persecution had
not as yet begun, for the spirit of Christianity was diametrically opposed to the life
of the Roman world. The characteristic
features of that life were carelessness and
indifference both in religion and in morality.
The Roman Empire knew no religion but
that of the gods of the state, chief among
which was the deified imperial power, but it
tolerated contemptuously all sorts of faiths
and beliefs, as long as they did not come in
any way in conflict with its authority.
Christianity might have had this toleration
if the Christians had been willing to accept

it, or willing to admit that their religion was on an equality with the many worships which surrounded them, and bow their head before the supreme divinity of Cæsar. But from the very first we find the Church without hesitation assuming the position that it alone possessed the truth and had a message to all mankind. Between two such positions, each of the bodies claiming universal authority, and demanding absolute submission, there was no possibility of reconciliation and compromise. No man could worship Christ and adore the Genius of Cæsar at the same time; and the Christian discipline, which forbade its members joining in the games and festivals which were so closely interwoven with all the life of the heathen, separated them distinctly from the world in which they lived, a world which they believed, and not without reason, was doomed to perdition. As a rule, the Christians did not court martyrdom, believing that our Lord had forbidden such action, but at a very early date a belief arose of the value of martyrdom as an offering to God, and of the

wonderful blessing of thus winning heaven
by a few sharp hours of suffering ; and
zealots were found who rushed upon their
fate, and goaded by insults even unwilling
magistrates into persecution, hoping to wash
away in their own blood the stains their
souls had contracted. But, though there
was some extravagance, Christian history
and tradition is full of the most pathetic
accounts of heroic constancy in the face of
awful suffering, where weak women and
children became strong in the might of the
Master whom they served, and overcame by
"his blood, and by the word of his testimony, and they loved not their lives unto
the death."

Few passages in any literature are more
inspiring or more touching than the letter
from the Christians in Smyrna telling of
the martyrdom of Polycarp, or the simple
narrative of the martyrs of Carthage contained in the Acts of Perpetua and Felicitas.
The aged bishop, the noble Roman matron,
the humble slave-girl, the boy catechumen,
all faced death and tortures with the same

patience and the same triumphant gladness
that they had been found worthy to seal
their confession with their blood.

When at last the storm of general persecution broke, it broke with force all the greater
because it had been so long preparing and
because the Christians had become numerous
enough to be feared as well as detested. The
emperor Decius was called to the throne in a
moment of the greatest danger to the empire.
Wild hordes of Germanic peoples, A. D.
long the most dreaded enemies of 249.
Rome, hosts of Goths and Franks, had entered
the provinces and were threatening the civilized world with destruction. In their extrem-
ity the Romans turned to religion, which for
ages had been little more than a formality
of state. They believed the gods were angry
at the impiety of the people, and that they
were showing their wrath upon the empire.
The temples were once more thronged with
eager worshippers, and all over the empire
an attempt was made to compel the Christians to forsake their faith. The blows fell
with the greatest severity upon the leaders

of the Church, who were sought out and punished as the chief offenders, and for several years the persecution raged, during the lifetime of Decius and his successors, Gallus, Æmilian, and Valerian.   The strain was very severe, and told upon the Church.   It drove from it many who had become Christians from taste rather than from conviction, and it destroyed many of the most prominent of the leaders.   But the great majority of the Christians were constant in their faith; and after the rage of persecution was spent, the Church arose all the stronger for the contest.   For forty years it was unmolested, and in fact is said to have received legal recognition as an allowed religion ; and in this period of peace the number and influence of its members increased rapidly. Once more, however, came a period of trial and of persecution, and this time the most widespread and severe of all.   In the civil disturbances at the beginning of the fourth century, hostile measures against Christianity were again undertaken.   The empire at last recognized fully the problem that

A. D.
251–260.

was presented to it by the existence within its limits of a society whose members owed allegiance to another Lord, and directed all its forces, not now to frighten Christians into conformity, but to extirpate the very name of Christianity. The Diocletian persecution struck at laity as well as

A. D. 303.

clergy, low as well as high, youths and women as well as men. All over the empire it raged for seven or eight years ; churches were destroyed, thousands of martyrs suffered, and the sacred books were sought for and burned with bitter malignity, until at last the triumph of Constantine put an end to the persecution. It was believed by the exulting Christians that on the eve of his most serious battle, on which his fate and that of the empire depended, the Emperor had seen in the sky the figure of a cross formed by the initial letters of the Saviour's name, and underneath the words τουτῳ νικα " By this conquer." Impressed by the vision, he ordered the Labarum, or cross-bearing standard, to replace the Eagles ; and when victory was his, with his associate Licinius, he issued

A. D. 312.

the edict of toleration that gave peace to
the bleeding Church.

Wonderful triumph of faith and constancy!
The little one had become a thousand, and the
small one a strong nation.   The Christian
Church had kept the faith and had overcome.
It had refused to be a Jewish sect ; it had
refused to be an oriental philosophy ; it had
refused to receive the toleration of the state
as one of many religions of the Roman world.
Convinced of its divine mission, full of its
precious message for mankind, it had kept
steadily in its appointed path, undeterred by
opposition, by ridicule, or by violence, and
now God had given the victory.   The new
and heavenly Jerusalem saw now the children
of those who had afflicted her come bending
unto her, and heard the name of her God,
which men had despised, now honored and
revered. · It is one of those stupendous events
in history which are inexplicable by purely
earthly considerations ; a witness beyond all
controversy of the ruling and guiding hand
of God.

Into the story of the Church's triumph I

shall not enter ; my subject to-day is rather of the struggle than of the victory, of the prayers of sadness rather than of the hymns of praise. There is no history so stimulating, no record of human events so noble, so little alloyed with frailty, weakness, or self-seek- ing, as is the tale of constant endurance and patience and faith and hope, that is told us in the story of the first three centuries. This is the heroic age of Christianity, the true romance of history ; and it is most surpris- ing that it is so little studied by Christian people, and that they are content to be unfamiliar themselves, and to allow their children to be unfamiliar, with the mighty deeds of our Christian worthies, who "wrought righteousness, obtained prom- ises, stopped the mouths of lions, out of weak- ness were made strong, waxed valiant in fight, turned to flight the armies of the aliens." There are few more impressive places in the world than the great Flavian amphitheatre in the city of Rome, conse- crated to the worship of God, as its proud inscription reads, by the blood of the martyrs shed within its walls. It has witnessed the most sublime, though the most cruel, scenes in human history. There the aged Ignatius, bishop of Antioch, second from the Apostle's time, was, as he himself phrased it in the striking metaphor, " ground fine beneath the teeth of the lions that he might be choice flour for his Master's granary." There those of whom the world was not worthy faced calmly the most horrible of deaths, and the still more horrible hatred that they could see upon the unpitying faces of Roman maidens and matrons, who came to see Christian maidens and matrons torn to pieces by wild beasts for their diversion. The noble heroism of the aged Polycarp at Smyrna, the constancy amid excruciating tortures of the martyrs of Vienne, the simplicity and sweetness of the faith of Perpetua and Felicitas, the manly fidelity of Lawrence, the dignified and triumphant death of Cyprian, all these and many others should be as familiar to Christians of to-day as the stories of their own land. Our heavenly commonwealth has its patriots as well as our earthly country, whose example may stimulate our weakness and shame our indifference. So, also, does it possess its statesmen, its great thinkers and writers, who have shaped the form of human thought, and by their clearness of mental vision have influenced profoundly the subsequent opinions of mankind. There are Justin Martyr and the other apologists, the first formal defenders of Christianity by written argument ; there is Irenæus, the great theologian of Lyons, the bulwark of the Church against the follies of the Gnostics ; there is that wonderful school of Christian philosophy at Alexandria, whose leaders, Clement and Origen, were the creators of Christian metaphysical thought ; there is Tertullian, the stern critic of his weaker brothers, the puritan of the early Church, like modern puritans carried by the severity of his temper into separation, yet without leaving hold of the great verities of the faith ; there is Cyprian, the great bishop of Carthage, who has left us his remarkable treatise upon the Unity of the Church, and who fought out in his day questions which still arise from time to time. The

literature of these centuries is indeed remarkable, both in its amount and in its breadth
of thought. We need not expect to find it
always sternly logical according to the formal
laws of reasoning. There is a directer logic
of which the Fathers were masters, the logic
of the heart rather than of the head. Their
methods of reasoning were at least better
than those of their opponents, and their
cause was better ; and if in our conceit we
sometimes smile at their argumentative
fallacies, the simplicity and reality of their
faith should bring us to our knees.

It is not necessary to enter into any discussion of early heresies and errors. There
are none of them that have more than a
historical interest, except as showing how in
all ages the tendencies of error are alike.
With the exception of one or two that arose
over questions of discipline, they were rather
travesties of Christianity than forms of Christianity.

Thus we may see how the Church grew,
from the few disciples in the upper room
to the time of her final triumph under Con-

stantine, by a natural process of growth, by the development of the divine life which it had received at the beginning. This development, like all development, was by a constant process of differentiation and specialization. In the first period, the Church was clearly separated from Judaism ; in the second period, from the Greek and oriental philosophies ; in the third period, from the religions of the Roman world. At first, its enemies were the Jews alone ; then Jews and philosophers both ; at last, all the powers of the earth. The organization of the Church was also a development, under the guidance of the Apostles and their followers, from the simple almost unorganized condition of the first little community in Jerusalem, to the completed episcopal system which was to be found everywhere by the middle of the second century. The doctrine of the Church was maintained by its organization. From the very beginning the Church has been the witness and keeper of Holy Writ. To the men of the second and third centuries we owe an immense debt of gratitude for their inestimable ser-

4

vices in collecting and editing the scriptures
of the New Testament. With a wonderful in-
tuition, most amazing in such an uncritical
age, they selected from the mass of writings,
the books which best deserved the consideration of Christians, recognized their divine
character, and established at once the practice, so indispensable to the Church, of read-
ing them regularly as a part of their public
services. This gave the early Christians a
wonderful familiarity with the words of the
New Testament, which entered into their
daily life and formed part of their daily
speech ; so that it has often been remarked,
that should the copies of the Gospels have
been lost, they might have been in great
measure replaced from the quotations in the
works of the early Fathers. By the divine
guidance the Church was led safely and tri-
umphantly through the first ages of its existence. The great first steps were taken,
never to be repeated ; the character was
formed, never to be completely changed.
Upon the one foundation that had been laid
once for all, wise master-builders had reared

the walls of the temple of God, and when the time of trial came, their work was made manifest, and the day declared it, because it was revealed in fire ; and as the apostle had foretold the fire of persecution proved the abiding and immortal character of the structure they had reared.

LECTURE II.

THE CHURCH OF THE CHRISTIAN EMPIRE.

LECTURE II.

THE CHURCH OF THE CHRISTIAN EMPIRE.

THERE is always some disappointment even in the greatest triumphs ; the attainment is never quite equal to the anticipation. The history of the Christian Church in its hour of victory forms no exception to this general rule. As a great modern writer has said : "This is a world of conflict, and of vicissitude amid the conflict. The Church is ever militant ; sometimes she gains, sometimes she loses ; and more often she is at once gaining and losing in different parts of her territory. What is Ecclesiastical History but a record of the ever-doubtful fortunes of the battle, though its issue is not doubtful ? Scarcely are we singing *Te Deum*, when we have to turn to our *Misereres :* scarcely are we in peace, when we are in persecution :

scarcely have we gained a triumph, when we are visited by a scandal. Nay, we make progress by means of reverses ; our griefs are our consolations ; we lose Stephen to gain Paul, and Matthias replaces the traitor Judas." *

The seeming success of Christianity was accompanied by serious corruption both in faith and practice ; its gains in numbers and in power were at the expense of much of its ancient strictness of discipline and simplicity of life and worship. Its history is not as inspiring as that of the first three centuries ; there is much more to tell of error and weakness, of sin and of folly, than in those early ages of heroic contest. The Church had passed the period of its childhood, with its simple virtues and simple faults ; the errors of its adolescence are more repellent, its very virtues less attractive, than those of its early days.

Yet it would be a great mistake to fancy that this was a period of apostasy, or devoid of much that was true and noble. As in

* Newman, *Historical Sketches*, III. 1, 2.

the times of persecution the violence of the world had failed to overcome the heroic resistance of Christ's soldiers and servants ; so now, in spite of the more insidious temptations of prosperity, the Church maintained the faith and held up a standard of morality incomparably purer than that of the world about it. If the virtues of Christians do not shine with the transcendent brightness that they did at first, it must be remembered that the background against which they appear is not the utter darkness of heathenism, but the half light of a general if imperfect acceptance of the principles of Christianity. The very fact that the general average was higher, will explain why the contrasts are less strongly marked.

In the age of the Christian empire may properly be included those centuries in which the empire was still the dominant world-power, before the Germanic tribes in the West, and Avars, Slavs, Bulgarians, and Arabs in the East, had broken up the time-honored unity of law and order which had been the gift of the Cæsars to the world.

In the West the catastrophe came in the fifth century, and although in the sixth century Africa and Italy were for a time recovered, the unity was never that of the former undivided empire. In the East the process of destruction was more gradual, but by the middle of the eighth century little was left to the empire beside a narrow fringe of coast around the Balkan peninsula and a few Greek towns in Asia Minor which were still able to hold out against all-conquering Islam. The principal ecclesiastical events of the period, both in East and West, may be included in the limits of two centuries from the time of the conversion of Constantine. After that time the Eastern Church almost ceases to have a history ; and though the history of the Church in the West is full of interest and importance, its characteristic features are so distinct that it needs to be considered by itself.

In this period, as in the preceding, we may see great dangers resisted and great advances made ; but the dangers, instead of being successive, were simultaneous, and the progress made became in its turn the cause of further dangers and difficulties against which Christianity is still struggling. The dangers arose from two sources, the connection of the State with the Church and the popularizing of Christianity. They assailed the Church in its faith ; and were met by the great ecumenical councils with carefully prepared definitions of Christian beliefs. They assailed the Church in its morals ; and were met and resisted by the growth of asceticism. They assailed the Church's liberty and independence of action ; and were met by the determined resistance of the prelates. Progress was made in definiteness of theological conception ; in the standard of life maintained by the best and noblest of the age ; and in the realization of the supreme dignity and honor of the Church's position. Yet definitions and creed-making tended to set theology above religion in the Christian consciousness ; ascetic virtues led to the irrational vagaries of monasticism ; and spiritual independence, when not crushed out as in the East, was perverted into ecclesiastical domination, culminating in the claims to absolute supremacy of the western papacy.

It is a confusing period to study, especially in the early and the later portions, as changes take place with such rapidity that it is like watching the bewildering variations of the kaleidoscope. It is full of great men, those most disturbing elements in historic generalizations, who do not move according to one's preconceived ideas and constantly compel one to throw aside some most alluring general conception. Yet by confining ourselves to the three points I have indicated, faith, discipline, and liberty, and holding to the threads that lead from them, it is possible to pass through the maze and to gain some idea of its strange bewildering fulness of life and thought.

I.

THE FAITH.

THE Church had hardly recovered from the blows of persecution, the wounds of the confessors had barely healed, when it was convulsed by theological controversy upon a fundamental doctrine of the faith, the nature of the Founder of Christianity.

The controversy broke out in Alexandria, which had been for many years the home of Christian theological thought. In revulsion from opinions that seemed to deny any real distinction between the Persons of the Trinity, a presbyter named Arius had preached and written most vehemently, using language which implied, if it did not actually express the thought, that the Son of God was a creature and inferior in nature to the Father of all. At first popular sympathy seems to have been upon his side. Converts from heathenism were more ready to accept this doctrine than the more mysterious faith of the Catholics, especially as it was urged by Arius as necessary to a belief in the unity of God, the primary article of the faith which they had accepted at their conversion.   When however it was demonstrated by the keen logic of Athanasius that the doctrine of Arius was necessarily ditheistic, making two Gods of different natures from one another, this sympathy began to disappear.

The victorious Constantine, when he had quieted civil dissensions and had made himself sole master of the world, found to his surprise that the Christianity whose unity had overcome the divisions of paganism was divided into hostile parties.   At first, he seems to have thought that the discord could be quieted by exhortation ; but when he found that this method of treatment only made A. D. 325.   the matter worse, he summoned a council of Christian bishops to meet at Nicæa in Bithynia to consider the matter.

The method of settling theological disputes by a council of bishops was not unusual in the Church. The bishop had grown to be considered as the representative of the church over which he ruled, and assemblies of bishops meeting for purposes of common conference were believed to be specially governed and guided by the Holy Spirit whom Christ had promised to his Church as a whole. Once before had Constantine summoned a council of bishops to meet, at that time in the West, to consider questions which distracted the Church in Africa. Arles, A. D. 314. The peculiarity of the meeting of Nicæa was that it was the first which was distinctly *general* in its character. Bishops were summoned from West and East alike ; and though nearly all the three hundred and eighteen who attended were from the East, yet all felt that it was a gathering more solemn in its character than any which had been held before it. Everything was done by the imperial officials and by the bishops who were at the court of the emperor, to make this first formal assembly of the spiritual rulers of the Christian empire as impressive as possible. The proceedings were opened

by Constantine in person, in all the majesty
of his imperial state, and he exhorted the
bishops to unity and harmony. It must
have been a most impressive gathering, for
there were assembled there the men who
held the highest station in the churches of
the East. The bishop of Alexandria was
there, with his quick-witted and brilliant
young archdeacon, the celebrated Athanasius; there was Arius himself, the madman,
the Libyan serpent, as his enemies nick-
named him, tall, ascetic, severe, and with a
peculiar nervous habit of twisting his body
and thrusting forward his head suddenly
when he was excited, that perhaps had
gained for him the uncomplimentary title.
There was the learned and courtly Eusebius
of Nicomedia, the friend of Constantine and
the great supporter of Arius, and there also
was the dignified Hosius from Cordova in
far-off Spain, who also possessed the confidence of the emperor, and used his influence
to oppose the designs of Eusebius. Others
were there who were famed, not so much for
their learning or position as for their sanc-

tity—confessors, whose halting steps and mutilated faces bore witness to the constancy with which they had kept the faith in the days of terror, under Diocletian and Galerius. These, though simple-hearted men of little theological attainment, were able to exercise great influence by the reverence their characters inspired.

The council, far from resenting the prominent part taken by the emperor in the proceedings, welcomed thankfully his mingling in the affairs of the Church, as giving the august sanction of the civil authority to their conclusions and resolves. Theoretically, they conceived the decision of such a council of bishops to be the voice of the Holy Spirit; but with a natural inconsistency pardonable in them, though of very evil import to the Church, they were glad to supplement the heavenly authority by earthly force. It was an amazing change, that might well have turned the heads of any men, for the Christian prelates to find themselves honored, respected, and even treated with deference, by the master of the world and by his serv

5

ants, who were quick to follow the imperial example.

The emperor, after formally opening the council, withdrew and left the discussion in the hands of the bishops. There was a general agreement that the negations of Arius were wrong and dangerous, but much difficulty was found in agreeing upon any form of belief that would exclude his error. A strong attempt was made by the friends of Arius to bring about the adoption of a creed which, though perfectly orthodox as far as it went, would have been broad enough to include both Arians and Catholics. This was vigorously resisted by the party of the bishop of Alexandria and at last a clause was added which asserted that the Son was *homoousios*, consubstantial with the Father, thus definitely pronouncing against the error which they condemned. Great difficulty was experienced in carrying this phrase, which was denounced as novel and unscriptural ; but the urgency of the emperor, who seized on it as the solution of the difficulty, prevailed upon the unwilling ; and it was accepted by all except Arius and two bishops who had been from the first his strongest supporters. They were condemned and disgraced, and the amended creed was promulgated with both conciliar and imperial authority, as the authorized belief of the Holy Catholic Church, the Church of the Christian empire.

In this way the attempt of speculative philosophy, with a rabbinical use of the words of the Scriptures, to impose its novelties upon the Church, was met and defeated; and the old traditional faith, with its new guarantee which the denials and negations of Arius had made necessary, was established with every sanction that Church and State could give it. Severe penalties were denounced against the upholders of the heresy, and the secular authority, which so recently had been engaged in attempting to uproot and suppress dissent from the established paganism, was now exercised in suppressing those, who though Christians differed from the form of Christianity that the empire acknowledged. This was an unfortunate result of the conversion of the empire, though one that was to have been expected ; and soon Catholics in their turn learned by experience that the supremacy of the State in causes ecclesiastical was as dangerous under Christian emperors as under pagan. For with a surprising rapidity, in spite of the decrees of the council, and the sacrosanct edicts of the emperor, the opinions of Arius seemed to spread and gain mastery in the East. The emperor himself was persuaded that the council had gone too far ; Arius was recalled ; the edicts were revoked ; and when Constantine died and was succeeded in the East by his son Constantius, all the imperial power was used to disseminate Arianism and to crush its opponents. "The world wondered," to use St. Jerome's words, "to find itself Arian." In the East, the heroic Athanasius battled almost alone for the faith, but he was driven from his see and compelled to live in exile in the West. Such was the first object-lesson the Church received of the results of the union of Church and State.

Yet, in spite of the apparent triumph of Arianism, its reign was only temporary. The struggle was a sharp one, but in less than fifty years from the death of Constantine Arianism was almost everywhere suppressed. Even at the time of its greatest success, the apostasy was not as general as it seemed. The Arian leaders could maintain themselves only by the use of ambiguous and misleading formularies, cunningly contrived to have an orthodox sound and yet be susceptible of a heterodox construction. "The ears of the people were more loyal than the lips of their teachers." Again, Arianism soon split up into two sections, one of which was offensively negative in its teaching, denying entirely the divinity of the Son of God ; the other was much more moderate, composed of men who had either been misled by the metaphysical subtleties of Arius, or who, without agreeing with him in doctrine, objected to the narrowing of the faith by new and unscriptural terms of communion. These latter were shocked at the blasphemy of the extreme men, and tended naturally to

approach closer and closer to the Nicene
formula.

In the less philosophic but more practical
West, the heresy never flourished, in spite of
the desperate attempts of the few bishops
who espoused it, and the efforts of the imperial power to bring about a forced unity of
confession.   During the lifetime of Constantine II., and of Constans, when the West was
politically separated from the East, the
Catholics were supported by the imperial authority ; and though, in the short period that
Constantius held the sole power, prelates of
prominence, such as Liberius of Rome and
Hosius of Cordova, were forced into submission, their action was at once repudiated by
the churches of Italy and Spain.   Thus the
Nicene formula, with its clear and definite
statement of the historic faith, had always
those who maintained and defended it, and
constantly received accessions from the moderate party in the East, who were driven to it
by the bald negations of those disciples of
Arius who were more Arian than the here-
siarch himself.   The division of the empire

between Valentinian and Valens emphasized the distinction between the parties, and the harsh measures of the Arian Valens drove many back to the faith which he persecuted. When at last he fell before the Goths A.D. at Hadrianople, the brave Spanish 378. general Theodosius became emperor in the East, and he threw his influence upon the side of the theology in which he had been reared. This brought the controversy to an end. A council was held at Constantinople in 381, and with hardly a dissenting voice the creed of Nicæa was ratified and promulgated once more as the authorized belief of Christendom. Deprived of secular support, Arianism passed away like a cloud, leaving however a bitter memory and an evil legacy of disputes and quarrels and of precedents for state interference. It survived only among the Germanic tribes, now pressing upon the boundaries of the empire, who clung to it with a national pride, as distinguishing them from the Romans whom they hated and despised.

Thus was ended the most serious struggle

for the faith that the Church had ever known, and it was ended with victory. Revelation, right reason, and tradition had met and vanquished a most dangerous assault from a half-converted philosophy and a wholly pagan scepticism. Yet, to win its victory, the Church had been obliged to define its faith more strictly and to trust to human phrases to defend its orthodoxy ; and it was not long before there were fresh battles to fight, and new definitions to make, to prevent misinterpretation of the form of words which now was accepted as the outward shrine of the faith. Philosophy did not give up its attempt to rationalize the Christian mysteries. For another century or more, new heresies kept continually arising in regard to the Person of Jesus Christ, and the Church was distracted with the struggles between the rival parties. Each victory of orthodoxy seemed to pave the way for an exaggeration of the doctrine vindicated, until it became itself a heresy. Thus Nicæa had condemned Arius for denying the perfect divinity of Christ ; Constantinople condemned

Apollinarius for the contrary doctrine of denying the perfection of his humanity. At Ephesus, Nestorius, the great patri- A.D. arch of Constantinople, was held 431. to have gone so far in maintaining the perfection of the humanity, as to throw doubt upon the completeness of the union of the divine and the human natures in the one person of the Saviour. They who condemned him were in their turn condemned at Chalcedon, for exaggerating their proper A. D. objection to the errors of Nesto- 451. rius into a denial of the distinctness and perfection of the two natures thus joined. Nestorianism can be seen to have been in its logical results a modified Arianism, while Eutychianism, as the heresy condemned at Chalcedon is called, was an error of the same nature as Apollinarianism. As these heresies arose they were met and condemned by general councils, and it is well for every modern Catholic to bear them and their results well in mind, for, though continually exposed, confuted, and condemned, the same errors continue to be re-invented from age to

age. One cannot do better than state the
summary of these events in the words of
Richard Hooker, the greatest theologian the
English race has ever produced ; words that
though familiar to all students of theology,
are not as generally known as they should
be :

" To gather therefore into one sum all that
hath been hitherto spoken concerning this
point, there are but *four things* which con-
cur to make complete the whole state of our
Lord Jesus Christ : His Deity, His Manhood,
the conjunction of both, and the distinction
of the one from the other being joined in one.
Four principal heresies there are, which
have in those things withstood the truth :
Arians, by bending themselves against the
Deity of Christ ; Apollinarians, by maiming
and misinterpreting that which belongeth to
His human nature ; Nestorians, by rending
Christ asunder and dividing Him into two
persons ; the followers of Eutyches, by con-
founding in His person those natures which
they should distinguish.   Against these there
have been *four most famous* councils : the

council of Nice, to define against Arians ; against Apollinarians, the council of Constantinople ; the council of Ephesus against Nestorians ; against Eutychians, the Chalcedon council. In *four words* ἀληθῶς, τελέως, ἀδιαιρέτως, ἀσυγχύτως, *truly, perfectly, indivisibly, distinctly* (the first applied to His being God, and the second to His being man, the third to His being of both One, and the fourth to His still continuing in that one Both), we may fully, by way of abridgment, comprise whatsoever antiquity hath at large handled, either in declaration of Christian belief, or in refutation of the aforesaid heresies."

The controversies of the sixth century were only modifications of these four great questions. Human ingenuity speculating upon transcendent mysteries would venture some rash inference as an article of faith, and would for a time bring confusion into the Church, but after the council of Chalcedon, in 451, there was little if any development of Christian doctrine, even in the way of explanation, and the most enlightened portions of the empire adhered with tolerable stead-

fastness to the formula then set forth. The
outlying churches in Syria and Egypt seem
always to have had a tendency to exaggerate
their favorite tenets into heresy. It may
have been from some peculiarity of race, or
perhaps from simple ignorance, or again it
may have been from a jealousy of the power
and influence of the great churches of the
two imperial cities ; but the fact remains,
that, from the fifth century onward, Jerusalem, where Christianity came into being, Antioch, where it first received its name, and
Alexandria, for so long the home of Christian
theology, came to be centres of error and
division. The Catholic faith was the faith
of the empire, and especially of the Latin
and Greek speaking countries. The weakening of the bonds that held together politically
the Empire and its outlying provinces was
manifested also in the Church.

II.

THE MORALS OF THE CHURCH.

HERESY was not the only evidence of the attempt of the world to destroy the Church. There was another and more insidious danger to be resisted, for heathen influence tended also to corrupt Christian practice and Christian morality. Superstitious practices which the early apologists had derided when used by the heathen, crept into the usages of the Church and were accepted as part of its system. It would have been impossible for the pagan world to conform itself to the austere Christianity of the second century; there were many more points of contact between the world and the Church in the fourth century. Multitudes now poured into the Church, following the example of their imperial master, and brought with them many of their old customs and old

ideas.   It cannot be denied that in this
period Christian practice lost much of its
old simplicity and conformed itself to the
lower standard of the world it had conquered.
Bishops, who became imperial functionaries,
were apt to pattern their manners after those
of their secular contemporaries ; and those
who rose to the charge of great patriarchates,
"wielded a power," as Newman says, "which
in times of external prosperity and in ordinary hands was too great for human nature."
The secular duties of the episcopate became so
numerous that it took the magnanimity and
the sanctity of great men like Athanasius,
Ambrose, and Chrysostom to overcome their
temptations ; and when they fell into the
hands of men "of coarser grain," it is not
wonderful that they produced a degenera-
tion in the conception of the spiritual duties
of the office.

The ceremonies of worship grew more and
more elaborate as the Church increased in
the wealth of this world ; the incense which
had been ridiculed by the apologists and considered to be the very symbol of pagan wor-

ship, now rose in clouds before the Christian altars. The use of pictures and images to aid devotion grew rapidly, and it was not long before practices essentially idolatrous crept into Christianity, and were excused or defended by the same arguments which had served the philosophic pagans in former days. The local shrines of nymph and demi-god, instead of disappearing utterly, were consecrated to saints and martyrs, whose intercession was considered as efficacious as had been the powers of the former possessors. The Virgin Mary, whose memory from the first had been held in profound respect, became the object of a reverence which recalls at least, if it is not actually derived from, the honors which had been paid to the goddesses of the old religions. In short, the pressure of the world upon the Church did much to destroy the high standard of simplicity and spirituality which had been the general characteristic of the Christianity of the first three centuries.

As heathen influence attacked the Christian faith in the form of heresy and Christian practice in the forms of superstition, so also did it assail Christian morality by attempting to reduce it to the old standards of the pagan world. The rush of half-converted heathen into the Church tended naturally to introduce into it many of the pagan ideas in regard to the conduct of life. Former periods of peace had always been accompanied by an increasing laxity of discipline and a lowering of the tone of the community; and now it was almost impossible for the Church to assimilate its hosts of new adherents without being in some degree at least assimilated to them. Various sects split off from the Church, from a desire to maintain by punitive measures the ancient sternness of discipline which the more practical minds of the great majority of the bishops saw was an impossibility. The Donatists in Africa and the Novatians all over the empire, much as they differed, were alike in condemning the laxity of the Catholics; but the uncompromising puritanism of the latter destroyed the influence that they might have had if they had been more moderate, and the zeal of the former soon degenerated into ignorant fanaticism. But though, from a wise leniency, the Church refused to go to the same degree of stern regulation of manners which had been possible in an earlier and simpler age, none the less did it protest most earnestly against the growing secularization and carelessness among its members. If it did not compel the ancient simplicity, it invited to it and held up before the eyes of the world an ideal of the religious life. The protest of the Church may be found in the rapid growth of monasticism and in the adoption of ascetic principles by all the great saints and leaders.

The origin of monasticism is obscure. It is probably an oriental practice which was borrowed or imitated by the Christians of the fourth century. The first Christian monks of whom we have any clear account were in Arabia and Egypt in the time of the last struggle between heathenism and Christianity, and the sanctity of their lives led to their example being followed in the next generation by many others. The fundamental idea of monasticism

6

was that of retirement from the world for the salvation of the soul ; nothing whatever—no natural ties, no circumstances of life, fortune, or position—being allowed to interfere with this one all-absorbing object. "It was not a question of this or that vocation, of the better deed, of the higher state, but of life and death. In later times a variety of holy objects might present themselves for devotion to choose from, such as the care of the poor, or of the sick, or of the young, the redemption of captives, or the conversion of the barbarians ; but early monachism was flight from the world, and nothing else. The troubled, jaded, weary heart, the stricken, laden conscience, sought a life free from corruption in its daily work, free from distraction in its daily worship, and it sought employments as contrary as possible to the world's employments, employments the end of which would be in themselves, in which each day, each hour, would have its own completeness ; no elaborate undertakings, no difficult aims, no anxious ventures, no uncertainties to make the heart beat, or the temples throb, no painful combination of efforts, no extended plan of operations, no multiplicity of details, no deep calculations, no sustained machinations, no suspense, no vicissitudes, no moments of crisis or catastrophe ; nor again any subtle investigations, nor perplexities of proof, nor conflicts of rival intellects, to agitate, harass, depress, stimulate, weary, or intoxicate the soul." *

It was this that gave the monastic life from the first its great attractiveness to men who were wearied with struggle. There they might die to the world, and obtain rest for their souls, in the calm simplicity of a life with but one object, one aim, one interest. There were also secondary objects of the solitary state : that the mind thus freed from worldly distractions might devote itself to prayer and praise ; that by self-denial, fasting, thirst, discomfort of every kind, they might mortify their earthly and corrupt affections, and thus fit themselves for the presence of God. Yet these, important as they were, were still subordinate to the pri-

* Newman, Historical Sketches, III. 375.

mary object—to escape from the world, in
order to flee from the wrath to come. Soon
the Nubian valleys, the Nitrian desert, the
defiles of Arabia, the barren uplands of Syria,
were covered with cells of hermits and communities of monks and nuns, who had thus
renounced the world, and had given themselves to what soon came to be called, by a
daring usurpation, the religious life. They
spread everywhere, and soon the black robe
of the monk was familiar in the crowded
cities as well as in the lonely wastes. All
the greatest men of the fourth century were
either monks themselves or patrons of con-
vents and monasteries. Basil, Gregory of
Nazianzum, Chrysostom, Nestorius, Epi-
phanius, Theodore, Theodoret, and perhaps
Athanasius, had all experience of the monastic life ; while in the West, Jerome, Cassian,
Martin, Pelagius, were monks, and Augustine and Ambrose, though not professed
themselves, were strong in their support and
encouragement of the system.

Monasticism uttered a protest, all the
louder because it was by deeds not words,

against the corruption of the age; and though it was abused by the idle and the ignorant and lost its original singleness of heart and aim, we should never forget what were the services it rendered by protesting, as it did, that the life was more than meat and the body more than raiment, and that there was nothing in all the world that a man could give in exchange for his soul.

The monastic movement exercised a deep influence over many who did not actually become monks or nuns. Its practices became the standards and ideals of the spiritual life, and were the desire and aspiration of many devout and humble souls, who were not able to profess the full monastic vows. Asceticism was indeed nothing new in the Church; the most earnest of the Christian teachers in the second and third century had urged its helpfulness and its beauty upon their disciples; and now the influx of worldliness was met by a great increase of ascetic practices and by a higher estimation of their value as an offering to God; and bishops and clergy whose duties kept them in the world, mothers

and wives, parents and children, who were
not able to obey the call of the votaries of
monasticism and cast aside the impulses and
affections God had given them, yet felt that
they should compensate for their worldly
position, or for their domestic happiness, by
chastening their bodies and mortifying in
some way their natural desires. Beautiful
as the idea was, it was liable to pass into
the grievous error that their bodies and their
affections were in themselves evil, and into
the still more erroneous belief that self-tor-
ture was in itself pleasing to the Almighty.
The idea of the superior holiness of the unmarried life had been growing in strength.
It was probably of heretical origin, but fell
in so thoroughly with the ascetic system that
it came to be very generally accepted ; and
Christians who married felt that their position was very inferior to that of those who
had preserved their single condition. A
most exaggerated estimate was placed upon
virginity, and a prurient sentimentality took
the place of the simple-minded and uncon-
scious purity of the earlier days of Chris-

tianity. The opinion spread rapidly through the Church that the clergy should live single lives ; and though, by the canons of Nicæa, those who were married before they were ordained were allowed to keep their wives, the tendency, especially in the sterner West, was towards celibacy. Fasts were frequent, and, with an idea that bodily discomfort was an offering to God, were multiplied by many of the most devout until they injured their health and wrecked their usefulness.

But with all its mistake and vagaries, asceticism was a useful and even a necessary protest against the profuse and shameless luxury of the age, which was the mock of moralists of every school, Christian and pagan as well. It was better for a man to starve himself, even to the point of injury, than for him to over-eat himself ; better to wear sackcloth and coarse garments than to lavish estates on his back, like the Roman nobles and ladies of whom both Ammianus and Jerome tell us, or the ladies in Constantinople who roused the indignant scorn of Chrysostom. It was better to live single,

better even to have absurd ideas about the
merits of celibacy, than to riot and revel in
the foul impurities which disgraced the daily
life of even Christian communities. When
we read the denunciations of the world by
some of the Fathers of this period, we are at
first shocked and scandalized at what seems
to be most exaggerated pessimism, because
we unconsciously apply the words to the
world as we know it to-day, which, though
it has much evil, is yet the better for fifteen
centuries of Christian training. When, on
the other hand, we realize how unspeakably
corrupt and evil was the world to which they
did refer, and which they knew far more
thoroughly than we can know it, we shall
have more patience with their seeming
extravagance. If we smile at the exaggera-
tions of ascetics, and deplore the false estimate of relative duties that they inculcated ;
if we condemn the sublime selfishness of
those who deserted friends, family, and position, for the sake of saving their own souls ;
we must still remember that it was asceticism and monasticism that bore witness, in

a way that even the blindest could see and appreciate, to the necessary union of righteousness and belief and to the supreme excellence and necessity of decency and purity of life.

III.

ECCLESIASTICAL INDEPENDENCE.

ONCE more, the world attacked the Church
by the union of Church and State, and by
the growing tendency in emperors and their
officials to interfere in the purely religious
province of the Church. By the conversion
of the empire a close connection was naturally and inevitably formed between the secular power and the Christian organization.
In fact, it was this compact organization, so
simple yet so effective, that had secured its
triumph. The bishops of the Church formed
a body with which the emperors could treat,
and the system possessed a unity that corresponded peculiarly with the well-subordi-
nated political unity which was the ideal of
Constantine and his successors. Little by
little the bishops became men of affairs,
almost imperial officials, until in the great

patriarchal sees they rivalled in importance the prefects themselves, the immediate representatives of the emperor. The desire of having the support of the State in the contests with paganism and heresy led to a subservience on the part of prelates that was doomed to bear a bitter fruit ; and emperors, from enforcing decrees of faith, passed readily into imposing them of their own will. That this was a pressing danger should be realized, for of all the evil legacies of heathenism, it has been most persistent and most apologized for ; yet it would be a most grievous mistake to imagine that the Church as a whole submitted willingly or generally to State interference. In the East, after controversy and heresy had exhausted the Church, the bishops sank indeed into little more than State officials ; but in the West, and also in the East during the period to which this lecture especially refers, the invasion by the State of ecclesiastical privileges was again and again resisted, with a boldness and a fidelity that recall the early days of persecution at the hands of the heathen. This age has its saints and confessors, as well as the former age of struggle ; and the spiritual leaders of the Church were always contending against the claim of the imperial power to dictate to bishops what they should believe and teach or whom they should admit to their communion.   Neither exile nor persecution nor

A. D.
296–373.

threats nor violence could daunt the heroic spirit of Athanasius, as he fought almost alone against the ruler of the world in defence of the faith of Christianity.   Neither threats nor blows nor exile nor lingering death could bend the resolution

A. D.
397–407.

of the brilliant and holy Chrysostom, who, like his namesake the Baptist, did " constantly speak the truth, boldly rebuke vice, and patiently suffer for

A. D.
374–397.

the truth's sake."   Ambrose of Milan bade a stern defiance to the commands of an Arian empress to surrender one of his churches to the heretics, and boldly rebuked the great Theodosius when, red with the blood of the innocent, he attempted to

A. D.
412–444,

present himself at the altar.   Cyril of Alexandria, little as are his claims to sanctity, was a determined opposer of the usurping authority of the emperor's agents, and won a battle for the Church, though with weapons that were unsuited to his holy office. Nor need more be named ; one can hardly read a page of the historians of the period without finding some instance of the resistance of the Church to the domination of the secular power. But the conflict was in itself a misfortune, for even where most righteous and necessary, contention and strife bear evil passions in their train ; the effect upon the character which came from contending for privilege or even for a proper independence of state control, was very different from that which had been produced in the previous century by the contest for the faith. Out of these contests arose the claims of spiritual prerogative, that made each see jealous of its neighbors and rivals, and finally led to the claims of spiritual supremacy which were raised by the bishops of the old imperial Rome.

Thus, though the world assailed the Church with threefold vehemence at the moment of seeming triumph, its assaults were met and resisted, and Christianity arose, bleeding and disfigured perhaps, but victorious, from the struggle. The attack upon the Christian belief was repelled by the heroic resistance of a few and by the quiet constancy of the many, and the faith was clearly and explicitly defined in the creeds of the four great General Councils of Nicæa, Constantinople, Ephesus, and Chalcedon. The attack upon the morality and spirituality of Christian worship and Christian life was opposed by the stern self-denial of asceticism and by the severe simplicity of monastic life and worship. The attack upon the Church's independence was fought out by a spirited resistance on the part of the leaders ; who, while honoring the Emperor as God's representative on earth in temporal affairs, refused to surrender the precious liberty of thought and action which was their Christian heritage.

No period in the history of Christianity is as rich as this in great men, whose lives and words have shaped the course of human affairs—great saints, great scholars, great preachers, great theologians. The stir of the times, its manifold and complex life, the greatness of its events, is reflected in the majestic figures of the Christian leaders. Ecclesiastical biography becomes a study of the profoundest interest, and we are most fortunate in possessing contemporary records of great value which, together with the voluminous writings of many of the great actors themselves, enable us to gain a vivid conception of their lives and characters. A period which comprises such men as Athanasius, Basil, Gregory Nazianzen, Chrysostom, Ambrose, Martin, Jerome, Augustine, to mention only a few of the most prominent, can hardly fail to be brilliant and full of interest. The individuality of the Fathers of the period is as striking as the strength of their characters and their sanctity. No two of them are alike ; each great soul had, as it were, its own special angle of polarization, for the transmission of the divine light which was the life of them all. In Athanasius we have the stern theologian, the gallant warrior, faithful among the faithless ; in

Basil, the sweet-tempered mystic, loyal and true to his appointed service, in spite of depressing illness, misrepresentation, and suspicion; in Chrysostom, the brilliant orator, the keen and sensitive spirit, which could spend and be spent for those he loved, but which was as resolute as that of Athanasius, when resistance was a duty. In Ambrose we have the majestic prelate, yet the simple-hearted servant of Christ, who took up the heavy burden of the episcopate, which had come to him against his will, and made it redound to the praise and glory of God. In Martin we see the devout soldier, the earnest missionary, carried out of himself by the love of the souls of sinning and suffering men; one of the most apostolic figures of the period, warm-hearted, enthusiastic, and spiritually-minded. There can be no greater contrast than between him and his contemporary Jerome, whom also the Church reveres as a saint; the brilliant, erratic, dogmatic scholar, the great exponent of monasticism by his pen, as Martin was by his example; the translator and com-

mentator of the Scriptures, constantly involved in controversy, never at peace or
quiet, a stormy character, as boisterous yet as
invigorating as the winds of March. One
worked in quiet, the other in the uproar of
the tempest, yet each did his work thoroughly
and well, and for the sake of the one Master.
And of them all there is none that we know
so well, or feel so near to us, as the great
Augustine, partly because his acute thought
has shaped the theology of western Christendom, more however because he has laid
bare before us his very soul, in that most
inimitable of all books, the "Confessions."
Brought into the Church in his mature manhood, after a youth misspent in heresy and
in sin, he was able to exercise an influence
in the Church, which was the more profound
because his convictions were the result of a
bitter experience of the emptiness and bar-
renness of a life without religion. His conversion deepened in him the sense of the
awfulness of sin as estranging man from
God, and of the helplessness of man without
the aid of the divine grace. So Augustine

7

became the great theologian and doctor of
the West, and his theology was built upon
the evangelical doctrine of man's need of a
Saviour.   With an earnestness which is unequalled, with a learning rarely surpassed,
with a rhetorical skill that few have ever
possessed in like degree, he devoted all the
powers of his soul, all the rich gifts of his
mind, all the strength of his body, to urging
the claims of Christ as the Saviour of mankind.   His system was one-sided, it is true,
but the value of the truth that he presented
so unceasingly is so inestimable that we
cannot wonder that it controlled his thought
and shaped his system of theology.   Like
his master Ambrose, he was an ascetic,
but his robust common sense and his very
theology, by the intensity with which it
gazed upon the redemptive work of Christ,
saved him from the error of attributing any
inherent merit to the mortification of the
flesh.   Asceticism to him was the natural
mode of life for a penitent sinner, not the
perfection of a saint.

There is a striking contrast between the

theology of the eastern, and that of the western or Latin Churches. The one was speculative and mystical, the other practical ; the controversies upon the mysteries of the Trinity and the Incarnation never took hold of the western mind. The straightforward Roman, strong in his sense of law, accepted the Nicene formula as final, and had little temptation to fall into error by over-refinement of thought. The " credo quia absurdum" of Tertullian expresses in its strong paradox the leading characteristic of Latin religious thought. It was not without good cause that the Roman Church was appealed to so often during the fourth and fifth centuries, by the contestants in the great theological struggles ; for, far from the strife of tongues, the bishops of the apostolic see of the West were able to steer a straight course by keeping their eye fixed steadily on the truth they had received. The same boldness and clearness of vision that enabled Leo of Rome to protect his people from Attila and from Gaiseric, enabled him to declare the faith in his celebrated letter to the council of Chalcedon, in which, with rare tact and logic, he picked his way between the rival heresies of Nestorius and Eutyches, by holding fast to the one great conception which formed part of the life of the Church then, as it had done for ages, that Jesus Christ was very God and very Man.

The western mind, when it speculated, preferred to dwell upon the relations of man to God; so that the one great western heresy which both Leo and Augustine opposed was that of Pelagius, who exalted the free will of man to such a height that he seemed to deny the necessity of the grace of God. The Roman devotion to order and law colored the theology of the West, and men's conceptions of the divine rule were shaped after the pattern of the imperial rule on earth with which they were familiar. The West had no genius for transcendental thought. Its mind required definiteness and clearness, and hence in the western theologians we miss the exalted thought and high-soaring reasoning of the speculative Greeks and Orientals. Its weakness was in a tendency to narrowness and to materialism; but it may be doubted whether any less definite faith than that of Leo and Augustine and their followers could have withstood the trials which the coming centuries were to bring upon them. At least we may see this, that while a great part of the intellectual East fell before the assaults of the simple and definite belief of Islam, the Churches of the West were able to convert their heathen and heretical invaders, and to set up a bulwark against which the Mohammedan victors dashed themselves in vain.

The period ends in the midst of trouble, sorrow, and anxiety; the barriers that had for so long held back the nations of the North were broken down, and the civilized world saw anarchy and chaos sweeping away those time-honored institutions which seemed to men's minds as parts of the very order of nature itself. The imperial government was destroyed in the western prefectures, and even in the East the circle was narrowing fast around the capital that Constantine had reared upon the Bosporus. But, unshaken and unchanged in all its great realities, though setting itself with new forms to meet new needs as they came, the Church stood steadfast and fearless, amid the wreck of systems and the ruin of the world. "The rivers of the flood thereof shall make glad the city of God," had been the prediction of the Hebrew psalmist, and, by its unchangeableness and its stability, in the midst of the constant flow of change and decay of all temporal power and authority, the Christian organization proved its right to claim that honored name.

It is a strange history, but one rises from its perusal with a stronger sense of the eternal truth and sureness of the promises of God ; and the words of David rise again to the lips : "The Lord sitteth above the waterflood, and the Lord remaineth a King forever. The Lord shall give strength unto His people, the Lord shall give His people the blessing of peace."

LECTURE III.

THE CHURCH OF WESTERN EUROPE.

LECTURE III.

THE CHURCH OF WESTERN EUROPE.

WE saw in the last lecture how hard it is for us to comprehend fully the history of the Church of the Early Empire; it belongs to a civilization that is entirely foreign to us, and its point of view eludes us. Our methods of thought are different from those of the Christians of Greece and Syria and Egypt, and it is only with an effort that we can put ourselves into sympathy with them. It takes a very vigorous exercise of the best trained historic imagination to enter into anything like a clear conception of a life so foreign and a mode of thought so strange. In spite of the attempts of transcendental philosophers to revive it, the thought of Origen and Clement, and even much of that of Chrysostom and Athanasius, can never be anything more

than an exotic in western Christendom.
Far different is the case when we come to the
consideration of the history of that great
Church of the West, which has shaped, colored, and inspired the whole of our modern
European and American civilization.   What
we are to-day, our habits of mind, our mode
of thought, the general character of our religious ideas—all is mainly due to its influence.   In spite of the present unhappy divisions of Christendom, there still exists a
western Christianity which is distinct from
the eastern type ; and its characteristics are
so persistent, that in all the sects and schisms
into which it is divided there are more points of
correspondence and union than of difference,
and Romanists and Protestants resemble
one another more closely than either of them
resemble their brethren in the East.   Much
as we differ from the Church of Rome and
protest against its modern dogmas and its
usurped authority, it is always a comforting
thought that our differences are much less
important than the truths we hold in common.   For the last four centuries the west-

ern Church has been divided, but these form but a small part of its history ; for a thousand years it was joined together in a close and vital unity, and accomplished a wonderful work in building up, out of the ruins of the past and the vigorous life of the Germanic peoples, a new and strong civilization, fuller and grander and with nobler aims than the old civilization which was swept away. While the Churches in the East either fell before the assaults of the Moslem, or grew decrepit like the decaying Empire with which they were too closely connected for their good, the Church in the West rose to its opportunities and, instinct with the creative spirit, converted once again a *chaos* into a *cosmos*, and reared upon the ruins of the imperial power a vast spiritual empire.

In considering so rapidly the leading events of a thousand years of endeavor, of work, of victory, and of failure, it is evidently necessary to fix our minds on some prominent points to guide us through the vast maze of attractive and fascinating detail ; and for this purpose nothing can serve us better than to observe with care :

1. The evangelization of the Teutonic tribes ;

2. The growth, dominance, and decline of the power of the Papacy.

These two subjects are closely connected and interwoven together, historically as well as logically ; they were mutually causes and effects, acting and reacting upon each other. The two great forces by whose joint work our modern society has been built up are the Germanic peoples with their strong race character, and Christianity with its vigorous organization as well as its inherent truth. When the convulsions of the fifth century seemed to have reduced the political condition of the western world to utter ruin, the see of Rome succeeded in making its own all that was most vital in the old imperial system, all that was the strongest in the spirit of the Roman people.　It reared itself upon the ruins of the ancient state ; it taught the new nations in the ways of civilization and religion, guiding and ruling them, as children are ruled and guided. At last, however, it came to consider that this guiding and ruling was the one essential thing, for which all else in the world existed ; it exercised the dominion which it had acquired, merely for the dominion's sake, and then the new nations, which it had taught and reared from childhood to adolescence, rebelled against being treated as children forever, and threw off its authority.

All are familiar with the fact, that in the fifth and sixth centuries of our era the Germanic tribes, which for several hundred years had threatened the empire, burst over its borders, and before them the weakened imperial organization fell prostrate. It is true that the collapse of the empire was a gradual process, but it was none the less complete. The slow stream of lava, that creeps along inch by inch, engulfs vineyard and village on the slopes of Ætna or Vesuvius, not less surely than do the showers of ashes and the fiery rain that bring destruction at once. Little by little the frightened world beheld over all the West the overthrow of the

old order, and the substitution, in the place
of system and law, of the arbitrary will
of the German war chiefs. Fierce Vandals
made the rich and prosperous Africa their
own, destroying and wasting its richness,
blasting its prosperity ; Goths, a shade less
barbarous, ruled at Toledo and Toulouse,
Cordova and Bordeaux. Other and nobler
Goths, at Rome and Ravenna, gave peace for
a time to plundered Italy, but were over-
thrown by the forces of the empire, only to
make room for fiercer and more savage Lombards. Wild Franks held the Rhineland and
the valley of the Scheldt, and soon overran
and conquered the rest of the ancient Gaul,
driving the Gothic chieftains from Aquitaine,
and subduing and assimilating the Burgundians of Dijon and Besançon. In Britain,
forsaken by the Roman legions, the blood-
thirsty and piratical Angles and Saxons drove
the christianized Britons from their populous
cities and fertile fields in the east and south,
and established, on the ruins of Roman and
Celtic civilization, a purely Teutonic savagery, which yet contained within it many

germs of progress and advance. In the fron-
tier lands, east of the Rhine and behind the
Alps, conditions were even worse ; for there
the tribes which had been hindmost in the
race were fighting savagely with one another
for the next chance at the spoils of the Empire. Everywhere was chaos. One conquer-
ing tribe was now in the ascendant, and now
another ; one would begin to establish some
rudimentary order, and take some first halting steps on the path of civilization, when
forth from the forest would pour some fresh
swarm of fur-clad warriors, hardier and
hungrier than the last, who would swallow
up their predecessors, and thus add one more
change to the bewildering confusion of the
times. One might well have asked, when
empire disappeared, and the majesty of the
Roman law was set at nought, whether there
could be any power stable enough to resist
the universal dissolution, living enough to
bring order again to the distracted world.

Though secular institutions were swept
away, the Christian Church survived the
storm. The waves of invasion swept power-

less about it; ill-treatment, brutality, barbarous violence, only strengthened it in its domain over the souls of men. It was the Church, not simply Christianity, that met and conquered the victorious barbarians; the Catholic Church, fully organized, a definite society, possessing an organic life, highly developed and specialized, with its clergy and its laity, with its traditional discipline, with its independent resources, its habits of general discussion and concerted action, its clergy already trained men of affairs, its monasteries as centres of religious life in the outposts, its wealth of traditions and of precedents—it was this highly specialized body that met the rude masters of the new world and bade them pause in their career of self-seeking, self-willed destruction; that taught them all they would learn of its high lessons; that restrained their wildness, curbed their madness and self-will, and endeavored to conform them to its own likeness. An unorganized Christianity (if we can conceive of such a contradiction) would have perished in the confusion of the times. The Churches of the East, highly organized as they were, failed to check the spread of Mohammedanism ; but in the West, fortunately for the faith, fortunately for human society, there was an organization of a stronger character, that was able to stand the strain and stress of the centuries of anarchy without yielding or breaking.

This element of strength was supplied, partly at least, by the peculiar position of dignity and importance which was held in the West by the bishop of the apostolic and imperial see of Rome. I say partly, for we should also remember the sterner and simpler character of Latin Christianity which I have already mentioned ; it had not been exhausted by theological controversy like the East, and religion had taken there rather the shape of a rule of life than of a form of orthodox belief. Yet it was this very practical character that made the Papacy a possibility, and that gave it power ; so that it became an instrument in the hands of God for the conversion of heathen Europe, and for the preservation, and transmission to a
8

new Teutonic civilization, of all that was most precious in the old order which was swept away.

From an early period the bishops of Rome had claimed precedence and peculiar honor for their see. This claim, which undoubtedly was the result of the great importance of the capital and of its strange influence upon men's minds even in its decadence, was based by them, and is still based, upon three assumptions, none of which has ever been proved, nor ever can be. They are as follows :—

1. That Christ gave St. Peter authority over the other apostles and the entire Church.

2. That St. Peter was bishop of Rome.

3. That the supposed supremacy of St. Peter was connected with the see of Rome, and descended to his successors in it.

On this insecure foundation is built up the whole fabric of the papal claims—an immense pyramid, it is true, but balanced upon its apex.

During the imperial age, these assumptions had been disregarded by the rest of the

Church, except when some bishop in difficulty with his metropolitan, or patriarch in trouble with the Emperor, wished to enlist the bishop of Rome upon his side ; but the claims were reiterated with a steadiness, each precedent was utilized with an adroitness, which show that from a very early period the popes had formed the fixed purpose of pushing forward their demands at every available opportunity. In this course they have persisted with a wonderful stability ; no backward steps have ever been taken, no claims ever withdrawn, but every opportunity of advancing them has been seized, with a tact that is amazing and with an ingenuity almost more than human. They would have us believe that they are as they have been from the beginning, that the Papacy dates from the apostolic age, if not from Christ himself. Yet we can count the steps in the growth of the amazing structure, from its small beginnings to its colossal majesty in the middle ages, as men count the rings of yearly growth in the trunk of some huge tree.

The claims were, as I have said, of an early date, and though unheeded were constantly reiterated, until men in an uncritical age began to believe that there must be some reality underlying the assumptions, and to pay special, though not exclusive, honor to the occupant of what came to be called the Apostolic See.   When the political importance of the city of Rome declined, and Milan or Ravenna became the imperial residence in the West, the bishop of Rome was left the most important personage in the deserted capital, and he began to take to himself and his office all the old historical prestige of the imperial city.   His diocese, which at first had been simply the district of the urban prefect—the city and the suburbs about it—was extended to cover all the territory governed by the imperial vicars in Italy, which corresponded nearly with the peninsula proper.   Then, little by little, the jurisdiction was extended : first, appellate jurisdiction only was claimed ; then this was construed to give immediate authority, till finally, in the last hours of imperial rule in the West, Leo persuaded the miserable Valentinian III., the last ignoble scion of the Theodosian house to extend by imperial edict the jurisdiction of the Roman bishop over the entire western empire. Thus, step by step, here a little and there a little, the papal claims had made good headway before the final catastrophe arrived, which, by destroying all general secular authority in the West, tended to advance the ecclesiastical authority that survived.

A. D. 423.

Most of the Germanic war bands, which overran the provinces and swept away the old machinery of government, were nominally Christians ; but their Christianity was of a very rudimentary character, and much colored by their old heathen beliefs. Moreover, they had been converted during the period of the Arian ascendency, and they clung to their heretical belief with great tenacity after it had died away in the rest of the empire, possibly from national pride and the fidelity to their own customs that was their striking characteristic. Their heresy distinguished them from the Romans

whom they hated and despised, and gave them
the chance of plundering the churches of the
orthodox.   Some, however, as the Franks and
the tribes which conquered Britain, clung to
their old belief in the gods of Valhalla.   If
the civilization of the world was not to perish
utterly, it was necessary that the heathen
should be converted and the heretics re-
claimed ; and the Church set itself to the task
with a missionary zeal that bore great fruit
for the coming ages.   Not everywhere was it
successful : the Arian Vandals and Ostrogoths
remained Arians to the last, and were swept
away by the arms of Belisarius and Narses,
A. D. 535-555. the generals of the great Justinian ; but the Visigoths in Spain
and the Lombards in Italy, after long struggles, embraced the Catholic faith and entered into communion with the see of Rome,
which thus became more and more the centre
of western Christianity.   The conversion of
the heathen nations was still more significant.
The savage Franks, in the midst of their
A. D. 496. career of conquest, espoused Christianity and took the form of faith

and discipline that their Gallic subjects taught
them, and were welcomed at once as Catholic champions against the Visigoths and Burgundians, whose heresy they proceeded to
extirpate with fire and sword. Assisted by
the sympathy of the Church, they won the
mastery of Gaul and became the greatest
power in western Europe, while the Church
by their help rose in power and importance.
It is needless to say that the Christianity
of these early Frankish chieftains was
of a kind that left much to be desired.
They were cruel, perfidious, and avaricious.
The kings had their harems of wives and
concubines; every sort of violence and
outrage was common, and, if punished, the
punishment was usually a greater outrage
than the original crime. Yet, in spite of all
this, their acceptance of Christianity made a
vast difference, if not to the first generation,
at least to their successors. They were now
in the road to learning, to civilization, to
advancement. Rudimentary as their Christianity was, it contained vital germs which
could and would develop into a glo-

rious life. It had the promise of a future, which their pagan faith could never have.

The Franks knew nothing, of course, of ecclesiastical history or of former controversies, and were ready to accept what their teachers told them ; and in this way claims of freedom from the control of the secular power, and of the supremacy of the Roman bishop, which better instructed imperial officials might have rejected, were received without question by the fur-clad kings, who now began to masquerade in tunic and pallium. A strange life indeed was that of the world in the sixth and seventh centuries ; ancient traditions, imperial law, savage customs, ecclesiastical precedents, municipal liberties, all mixed up in bewildering confusion ; yet through it all we can discern one leading fact, that the only power that was strong enough and brave enough to restrain in any degree the brutal selfishness of the lords of the land, or to defend and plead for righteousness and justice, was the Church of Christ. It surely is not amazing that, in the midst of such difficulty and danger, the isolated churches in the barbarian kingdoms should have sought to strengthen their own position by drawing closer and closer to the Roman See.

Our own forefathers in England were still more savage than the Franks. They obliterated the old Christian civilization in the greater part of Britain, and drove the Britons who had refused to submit to them into the mountains and moors of Wales and Cornwall. Churches were destroyed, priests slain at the altar, the worship of Woden and Thor and Freya supplanted that of the Christian's God. For a century, in the convulsions that racked the whole of western Europe, Britain and its woes were lost sight of ; but when at last the condition of Christian Europe became settled enough to allow men to think of other miseries than those immediately around them, the devout shuddered to think that a land, once consecrated to the worship of the Almighty, should be given over to savagery and paganism. There was no chance that England would receive

Christianity from the conquered people, as
had been the case in Gaul. The two races
were bitterly hostile ; the English had no
desire to be taught by the Welsh whom they
looked down upon, and the Welsh Christians,
in their turn, rather rejoiced at the thought
that in a future life they might hope to see
their successful oppressors burning in hell.
Teutonic England was to receive its Christianity from without ; to learn the truths of
the Gospel, as the first heathen had learned
them, from devoted missionaries, not to take
them as a part of the civilization of the conquered people among whom they dwelt. The
mission of Augustine to England marks the
beginning of modern missionary enterprise,
and was undertaken as a work of faith by
the wise and holy Gregory I. of Rome. It
was an enterprise of danger and devotion ;
when the missionary party were half-way to
their destination, their hearts failed them,
and they sent to the Pope to beg that he
would release them from their perilous under-
taking. Our ancestors bore a bad character
for cruelty, and the Italian monks whom

Gregory had chosen shrank not unnaturally from the unknown terrors of the strange land and the rude barbarians among whom their work would lie. But Gregory would hear of no drawing back, and encouraged them to persevere, and their success was remarkable. Kent, at that time the most powerful of the kingdoms A.D. 595. in England, soon yielded to their efforts ; and Augustine was created by the Pope archbishop and metropolitan, the first new bishop and metropolitan since the imperial organization had fallen in the West.

But it was not to the Roman missionaries alone that the conversion of the English was due. Their work was confined at first to the southern portion of the island, and was not entirely successful there, as a heathen reaction took place after the death of Augustine, that almost wiped out the new Christianity. The north and centre of England, with the Scottish lowlands, were led to the Gospel by the loving labors of monks from Iona, the disciples of the apostolic Columba, who had brought with him from

Ireland the old traditions of the Church in the sister island. Questions soon arose between the missionaries of the two schools. One side represented the fresh vigorous Christianity of the new Europe that was springing into life ; the other, though identical in all the essentials of the faith, clung with an affection that was almost schismatic to a few local peculiarities which they exalted into matters of principle. The clergy of the northern obedience have frequently been represented as resisting heroically the interference and intrusion of the Roman see. They deserve no such credit. They did indeed contend with it, and with the men who respected it so much that they had little patience with those who differed from them, but their resistance sprang not so much from any deep principle of ecclesiastical independence as from a desire to perpetuate the trifling differences which they preferred to the general consent of western Christendom. They were fortunately compelled to yield, and English Christianity came gladly and readily into full and close communion with

the great see of Rome, from whence English people had first received the   A. D.
Gospel. The harmonizing of the   664.
different sections of the Church was the
work largely of Theodore of Tarsus, who
became archbishop in 668, and united and organized the scattered missionary centres
into a strong and well-ordered society,
which by its unity and efficiency gave to the
discordant secular bodies a living example
of the advantages of union and organization. The conversion of England added
much to the prestige of the Papacy. It was
the first conquest of a purely heathen land,
and the English were grateful converts.
Soon, from the newly rescued island, missionaries were on their way back to Friesland,
to men nearly akin to them in race, and
even to the wilder heathen Franconians and
Thuringians on the eastern side of the
Rhine.

They carried the gospel, and with it respect
for the Roman see and the centralized system
of the Church ; and soon the Northumbrian
Winfrith became Boniface, the apostle of the

Germans, the great archbishop of Mayence. Thus England and Germany, brought from darkness to light, both served to enhance the importance and authority of the Pope. Their conversion had been mainly due to the Papacy, and they repaid it with their heartiest support against the disintegrating tendencies of the nascent feudalism which was beginning to develop itself among the Franks and Burgundians. One step more followed in the same sequence. Boniface, the English missionary, led the Frankish chieftain Pippin to seek, in a critical period, from the Church and the Pope, the help he needed for the political revolution that he contemplated ; and thus a new Frankish dynasty was established in Gaul, more thoroughly Teutonic in blood and in thought than that which it supplanted, powerful enough to check disintegration, and committed to the A. D. 752. support of the papal see. The new kingdom became great and powerful ; and then the popes conceived the idea of a still greater revolution, to throw off the shadowy bands that yet held them to the distant and decaying Eastern power, and to place a German prince, devoted to their cause, upon the throne of the Cæsars. In this way, they reasoned, the ancient imperial character of the Church would be restored, and the grateful barbarians would recognize and support the authority of the great potentate from whom they would have received the diadem. Charles, or Charlemagne (to give him the name by which the world has usually known him), the great and victorious king of the Franks, the unquestioned master of the greater part of Europe, the friend and bene- factor of the Holy See, was solemnly crowned at Rome, " the Mother of Empire," on Christ- mas day in the year 800, and men fancied that the rule of the Cæsars was restored, never again to be interrupted. A. D. Once more the world had come 800. back to its natural order, and now, with an emperor to be the secular head of Church and world and the Pope to be the spiritual head, all would go well. The mediæval idea of this joint rulership was,

that the world was committed to the care of
two chosen vicegerents of God : the emperor
to rule in secular affairs, and the Pope in
spiritual affairs.   In the ecclesiastical conception of the relation between the two
powers, it was held that as the sun is greater
than the moon, so is the Pope greater than
the emperor ; as man's soul is higher than
his body, so is the ecclesiastical rule higher
and holier than the secular.   But, unfortunately for the ecclesiastics, the new emperor
took his new position with a most serious
sense of its responsibilities and duties, and
treated his office as a gift from God, a solemn
trust in which he could have no partner nor
associate.   Full of reverence and respect for
the Pope and the papal office, he yet never
yielded any authority or precedence to him,
and the Papacy discovered that it had created
for itself a master, rather than an agent.
Yet, none the less true had been the instinct
which had led it to revive the empire, for
the new imperial organization, with its centralized system, developed in the growing
consciousness of Europe a sense of its natural

unity, which had been obscured, if not utterly
lost, in the chaotic centuries which had elapsed
since the last Cæsar laid aside the robe and
the sceptre ; and, moreover, the conception
of the Roman Church, as the church of
the Roman empire was clear, distinct, and
intelligible.

The triumph of the Papacy was deferred.
Charlemagne allowed none to be master but
himself, and after his death a second period
of confusion followed, which broke up the
new-found unity of the empire and prevented
it from ever becoming an universal government of Europe. A succession of able popes
for nearly a century enabled the Papacy
to make capital out of the dissension and
weakness of the State, but it also caught
the spirit of the age and, with the growth of
feudalism and the triumph of individualism
in Church and State, it declined. The fatal
gift of the temporal power corrupted its mo-
tives and debased its ideals ; not only did it
lose its power and authority, but it degenerated in piety and morals. Men of abandoned
lives were shamelessly raised to the papal

9

throne, and, while their claims were pushed with a zeal that surpassed all former efforts, the world was scandalized to see one who called himself Christ's representative on earth, a worthless reprobate. The forged decretals, which appeared in this period, seem to have been drawn up as weapons against the recalcitrant secular princes, and though frequently disregarded they were never withdrawn ; once put in circulation, there was no critical skill that could expose them, and each new forgery was used as a source from which most sweeping deductions could be drawn. When codified by Gratian in the tenth century, these forgeries, together with a nucleus of genuine letters of early popes, formed the body of the canon law of the Church.

After more than a century of confusion, rendered still more confused by the continued assaults of Norsemen and Saracens, something that approximated to a settled condition of society was at last evolved, though it was only the armed truce, and legalized anarchy, that we know as the Feudal System ; with the settling of society came also a desire for reform in religion. Monasteries were reformed; new and stricter orders were established; men began to go upon pilgrimages to holy places in the hope of atoning for the many sins of violence they committed at home; throughout Europe there was a remarkable awakening of the religious consciousness. This has sometimes been attributed to the existence of a superstitious belief that the world was to come to an end at the thousandth year from the birth of Christ, but there is no sufficient proof that this was a general belief, and the revival may be accounted for by the working of simpler and more rational causes. The world had been struggling for order and for peace; and when in the tenth century some little improvement was visible, the Church made use of the first signs of a better spirit, to push onward with renewed strength the battle for righteousness and holiness of life which it had always maintained, even in the midst of the fiercest disorder.

Rome, which had sunk the lowest, was

the last place to be reached by the wave of
reform ; but finally the vigorous German
princes who had revived the imperial power
and name in Germany and Italy, were able to
cleanse out the abominations at which all
Christendom was disgusted, and to restore
the papal see to decency and influence once
more.   In an amazing manner, which proved
the power yet exercised by the mystic name
of Rome, it regained speedily its ascendancy,
and gathered into its hands the leadership in
the work of reform, taking the movement
away from the laymen and pushing it to
lengths undreamed of.

The creator of the mediæval Papacy was
the celebrated Hildebrand, one of the most
remarkable men that ever lived.   In a subordinate station he ruled and guided the
policy of the Holy See for years before he
himself was elevated to the pontificate by the
A. D.   name of Gregory VII. ; and when
1073–1085.   he at last assumed the triple crown,
he boldly set himself to the work of making
the Papacy the supreme authority in the
world.   His efforts were especially devoted

towards the attainment of two objects closely connected with each other :—

1. To reform all existing abuses in the Church by the authority of the Roman see ;

2. By means of the reform, to put the Church at the head of all the true life of Europe.

Chief among the abuses at which he struck was the marriage of the clergy. This practice, which had become common both secretly and openly, he considered not merely unlawful, but a fearful and sacrilegious sin ; and he probably also saw what power the Church would gain if her clergy were celibates, separated from the world by the renunciation of the common ties of life, and devoted as a class to the one all-absorbing object of advancing the Church's cause. With an unmarried clergy there was no danger of the priesthood sinking into the condition of an hereditary caste ; on the contrary, it would need to be continually recruited from without with the best blood of the laity, and thus a constant and vital connection would be kept up with all conditions of society. The peasant, the burgher, the noble, all would be drawn close to the Church in which their sons devoted and consecrated their lives to holy offices.

Such a body as this would lend itself to organization, and the Pope believed that to secure the rule of morality and order on earth the Church must rule, and to secure the Church's rule its organization must be strongly centralized. As Guizot points out in his brilliant lecture upon this period, Hildebrand committed two great tactical errors : he laid out more work than it was possible for any man to accomplish ; and he proclaimed too loudly his intentions and desires. Both of these, it will be noticed, are the faults of an honest enthusiast who, strong in his personal conviction of the righteousness of his cause, considered concealment of his purposes or moderation in his desires a want of faith in the triumph of God. His measures soon brought him into conflict with the emperor, and long and eventful was the battle of giants. At one time, the lord of the world, as men deemed him, was obliged to stand in the garb of a penitent in the snow-covered courtyard of an Apennine castle, until the Pope was willing to take pity on his humiliation and to admit him to his presence to make there his abject submission. Again, the world saw with horror the sacred city stormed and sacked, first by the German troops of the emperor, and then by savage Norman supporters of the Pope. The emperor, deserted by his friends and betrayed by his own children, rested at last in an unblessed grave, while Gregory was driven from Rome to Salerno, and passed away with the sad words on his lips : " I have loved righteousness and hated iniquity, therefore I die in exile." The quarrel continued to rage between their successors, and though on minor points a compromise was reached which enabled each side to claim a victory, yet the solid fruits of success fell to the popes, who had generally represented the cause of order and justice, as opposed to the arbitrary wilfulness and selfish tyranny of the temporal rulers.

The Crusades, which were at once a direct

result of the religious revival of the period
and also of the more settled social condition
of Europe, served greatly to increase the
power and authority of the popes. They
were holy wars, undertaken at the bidding of
the Church, and under the special benediction
of the Papacy. The legates of the Pope represented him among the leaders in the field.
He was the advocate and protector of the estates and families which the warriors of the
Cross left behind them, when they journeyed
to reconquer for Christianity the sacred soil of
Palestine. The religious enthusiasm which
these romantic enterprises inspired was skil-
fully worked upon by the papal court for its
own advantage, so that before the Crusades
were ended the Pope was beyond all question
the mightiest of all European powers, ready
to give law to king or emperor and able to en-
force his decrees by the terror of his spiritual
censures. Kingdoms were laid under in-
terdict for the faults of their rulers ; monarchs who would not listen were chastised
into submission. One king of England was
driven to expiate his offences by kneeling

humbly to receive on his naked back the
blows of scourges wielded by exultant priests;
another was compelled to surrender his crown
into the hand of the Pope's ambassador and
to declare himself the vassal of St. Peter.
In the pontificate of Innocent III.   A. D.
the Papacy reached the summit of   1198–1216.
its power and authority. It humbled John of
England and Philip Augustus of France, and
saw the overthrow of the schismatical Greek
empire at Constantinople and the establish-
ment there of an emperor and a patriarch of
the Latin obedience. Never before had mortal
man achieved, or even aspired to, so high and
so awful an office. Supreme above all earthly
potentates, head of the Church on earth, vicar
of Christ and vicegerent of God—such a position required indeed omniscience and infalli-
bility. No fallible man, subject to the usual
conditions of humanity, was fit for such an
elevation ; and keen logicians, boldly seizing
the horn of the dilemma, began to assert that
the Pope must be infallible.

Many circumstances had combined to make
the papal power so tremendous. All the

learning and science of the day was in the
hands of the clergy ; they alone possessed the
keys of knowledge, as they held the more
threatening keys of discipline. The Church
had advanced while the State had stood still
or had been engaged in destructive and
suicidal conflicts ; and in the midst of the
struggle of the time, the clergy felt that in
honoring and supporting the Pope they were
honoring and sustaining the cause of right,
of justice, of enlightenment, and of progress,
as well as maintaining their own positions.

The Church attracted all the men of intel-
lect and mental power, who were not condemned by their birth to be secular princes,
and she welcomed these when, weary with
struggle and defeat, they threw aside the
helmet for the cowl, the sword for the cruci-
fix, and entered into some monastery to end
their days in peace and holiness. The new
universities which were beginning to spring
into life were at this time not only strongly
ecclesiastical, but especially devoted to the
Pope, as being able to free them from the
interference of the local authorities. The

new mendicant orders, Franciscan and Do-
minican, were preaching the gospel of life to
the poor as it had not been preached for ages,
building up thus a conscious and intelligent
populace in place of the serfs and hinds who,
little better than beasts, had tilled their masters' fields ; and these were bound by closest
ties of loyalty and affection to the popes from
whom they had derived their privileges, and
became their militia and recruiting officers
for their cause in every land. The Papacy
had made a bold stroke for power, wonderful
in that age in its statesmanlike sagacity.
It humbled the exalted and exalted the
humble. It made war upon kings and princes,
and was able to compel their unwilling submission because it had upon its side the great
mass of the people in every land of Europe.
The one office that was above all worldly
offices was one that might be attained by any
baptized man. Thus the democratic character of the Church of the middle ages was
the secret of its strength. When it declined
from this, when it lost the purity of its ideals,
and sought shamelessly for gold and power

and territory, after the fashion of the princes of the world, then it became as one of them in its actions as in its desires ; and its fall from its high estate was rapid and irrevocable.

The Papacy had said in its heart, as did the proud king of the ancient Babylon, "I will exalt my throne above the stars of God, I will ascend above the heights of the cloud, I will be like the Most High." The punishment of Lucifer followed, and the period of unequalled majesty and glory was followed by dishonor, shame, and disrepute.

As many causes had combined to place the Papacy upon its pinnacle of power, so many combined to drag it down when that power was misused. It paid the penalty of too ambitious an aim ; to sustain the ideal which had presented itself to the eyes of a Hildebrand or an Urban, it had exalted itself beyond the capacity of man ; and when the ideal was lowered, and human greed for gold and fame substituted for the nobler ambitions for the glory of God and the spread of His kingdom, it fell before the inevitable rebellion of right thinking men, who recognized that its eye had been turned from heaven to the things of earth. The men of the middle ages would have supported the Papacy if it had been true to itself ; its fall was its own work.

In still another way had the popes prepared their own downfall. They had humbled and weakened the empire, and by so doing they had weakened themselves ; for the new nations that were rising into prominence cared as little for religious as for political unity. With a strongly united Europe, a centralized Church under a spiritual emperor at Rome was an easy and natural conception. To an Europe made up of discordant and jealous nationalities, the task of preserving an ecclesiastical unity was too difficult. Revolution was sure to come, and the break-up of the unity of western Christendom was assured from the time when the Papacy first fell from its high position, in the beginning of the fourteenth century, though the law of inertia and the popular conservatism prevented any actual separation for over two hundred years.

Again, the partisans of the secular power, in the contest which broke out in the thirteenth century, were no longer unlearned as their forerunners had been in the eleventh. The old Civil Law of Justinian, with its sharp distinctions and purely intellectual conclusions, had been unearthed ; and its precepts, imperial as they were, framed for an utterly different society, were applied by the jurists to each half barbarous king, and every possible logical consequence deduced to the advantage of the secular power. The universities, unmindful of the Papacy's claim to their gratitude, were fast becoming secularized and the home of a sceptical philosophy. The very Franciscans and Dominicans were not always to be relied upon. The world, thanks to the more fixed condition of society, was growing in wealth and in knowledge. Learning was extending to the laity, and the methods of ecclesiastical government and administration, which had been a support to civilization in its earlier struggles, now became fetters and shackles for the expanding life of modern Europe.

One by one, the new nations, which, now the empire had been humiliated, were the leading powers in Europe, turned against the papal tyranny, and compelled it to exercise its dominion with moderation, as the only condition on which it could be allowed any authority at all. Saints, like Louis of France, and stern warriors, like the Edwards of England, were alike in checking the papal ambition and regulating its relations with their clergy and people. England, the vassal kingdom of the Papacy, not merely threw off all feudal allegiance, but, by the statutes of *Provisors* and *Prœmunire*, forbade the exercise of any papal jurisdiction in England without the king's consent.

When Boniface VIII. in his quarrel with the godless and faithless Philip the Fair of France, attempted to wield the thunderbolts of Innocent and Gregory, he found them powerless in his hands ; and the world saw with indifference the imprisonment and death of the pontiff. Then followed A. D. that period of humiliation in the 1303. annals of the Papacy, which is commonly

known by the name of the " Babylonish
Captivity," when, for seventy years, the
popes were compelled to dwell at Avignon,
within easy reach of the king of France and
his forces, and obliged to submit to all his
commands. When at last they freed themselves and returned to Rome, the Great

A. D. Schism broke out ; and Christendom
1378. was shocked and scandalized at the
sight of two, and at one time three popes,
each claiming to be the only genuine vicegerent of God and cursing and excommuni-
cating his opponents and their adherents.
The religious consciousness of Europe rose in
indignation, and a series of so-called general
councils attempted to restore peace and
order. These councils ended the schism, but,
unfortunately, their members could not free
themselves from the idea of the necessary
existence and authority of the Papacy ; their
efforts only tended to lift it from the prostrate condition in which it lay, and to give it
a fresh lease of life. Reform in the Church
was prevented, and the same abuses which
had scandalized right feeling men continued,

and were supported by the popes, who now sunk to the level of Italian princes, existing by the toleration of Europe, which desired an infallible spiritual head, but was careless and indifferent as to his private vices so long as his election and consecration was regular. Shamelessness of life, unblushing simony and nepotism, characterized the rehabilitated Papacy, until in Alexander VI. (Borgia) and in Julius II. it seemed to have sunk so low as to lose all claim to the respect of Christian people. Still, the institution was a venerable one, and men could not see, as yet, that the Church could safely dispense with it as a visible centre and mark of unity. All attempts at peaceful reform failed. The councils had failed; the secular princes failed when they tried to effect reform by their edicts and pragmatic sanctions. The court of Rome was far too clever for them, and their well-meant attempts came to nothing. Bolder spirits, like Wiclif in England and Huss in Bohemia, attempted reform by popular movements, unsupported by either secular or ecclesiastical authority; but the one

10

was silenced, and the other burned at the stake as a heretic. The Renaissance came with new intellectual life and new light, but throwing a deceitful glamour over the beauties of the ancient paganism. Scepticism and unbelief were rampant among the laity and the clergy as well. The Church, as a whole, set itself against the new learning, and it seemed as if the brilliant thought of the new age was destined to develop entirely apart from religion. The Church was in danger of utter destruction; it was losing its grasp upon the intellects and consciences of men. Reform in head and in members was indispensable if it were ever again to speak in the name of Christ to the world.

Such a condition of the Church, when all men were growing daily in knowledge and intelligence, was unendurable, especially to the few who were advancing also in devotion and true religion, who were applying the new light to the old problems, and were learning, from the revived study of the word of God, what were indeed the essential truths of Christianity. Reform was refused, abuses continued ; those who spoke against them were persecuted ; at last, the natural consequence of this repression followed, and produced in the sixteenth century that great revolution against the whole mediæval system of thought and discipline, that we call the Protestant Reformation.

The Hebrew story tells that when Baal worship seemed to have rooted out the worship of Jehovah from the land of Israel, and all resistance to have perished, the Lord revealed to the prophet, who deemed himself the only one left true to the old faith, that He had yet reserved Him seven thousand men, who had not bowed the knee nor kissed the image. In like manner, in spite of the corruption of the papal court and the frightful immorality of the monasteries, the scepticism of the learned and the superstition of the ignorant, there were always men who were quietly doing the work of God, who were praying earnestly, and preaching plain and simple truths, who were finding help in the sacraments and blessing from the word of God.

There was **never a** time when the comforts
of religion were **not,** to some at least, the
joy of youth, the stay of manhood, the con-
solation of infirmity, the hope in death.   The
sacraments still, in spite of all superstition
in regard to them, were ever telling of the
Father's forgiveness and of the Saviour's love,
and men were taught to look up and away
from the sufferings of this present world to
a future glory.   A history might be written,
that should contain only the record of progress and advance ; and when we praise, as
it is right we should, the men who were bold
enough to break with the tyrannical system
that had grown up around religion, and
to reform the shocking abuses which the
evil passions of men had brought into the
Church, we should remember that they owed
their religious training to men who had
gone before them, and that they had been
fitted for their great and important work
in the mediæval Church that they reformed.
" Vixerunt fortes ante Agamemnona."
There were devout and earnest Christians
before Luther or Calvin, Cranmer or Ridley;

the "Gospel" was not a discovery of the Protestant Reformation.

Thus, step by step, by gradual evolution, shaped slowly by changing age and circumstance, the Christian Church advanced in its path of progress. Ecclesiastical rivalry and ambition raised the Papacy at the very time when it was needed to render the organization of the Church adequate for the conversion and civilization of barbarian Europe. The barbarian nations, in their turn, grateful for the teaching they had received, raised him who had taught them to the loftiest position mortal man has ever held. When, intoxicated with power, the popes abused their awful office, the eyes of men were opened to see how slight was the basis on which the tremendous edifice was reared ; and the same Teutonic peoples whom the Papacy had trained, and whose support had made the papal power supreme, now cast it down from the throne it had usurped. The revival of religion in the eleventh century had raised the Pope to be in reality the ruler of western Christendom. It remained for the revival of religion in the sixteenth century to sweep away the remnants of a power that had become an anachronism, and to reconstruct an ecclesiastical system on a truer and more liberal basis.

LECTURE IV.

THE REFORMATION IN WESTERN EUROPE.

LECTURE IV.

THE REFORMATION IN WESTERN EUROPE.

THERE is an old Jewish proverb with which the members of that marvellous race have comforted themselves in many a period of oppression : " When the tale of bricks is doubled, then comes Moses." It expresses the common belief in the justice of Providence and in the righteousness of the divine government of the world. Abominable evil will work out its own destruction, unlawful tyranny is sure to bring about its own downfall. God is not always upon the side of the strongest battalions. Humanity in the long run thinks and reasons rightly, and may be trusted not to acquiesce forever in what its consciousness shows is false.

In the fifteenth century it seemed, indeed, as if evil had gained the victory both in Church and State, in the countries of western Europe.   In the State, the old ideas that had ennobled feudalism, ideas of rights and duties, of sacred responsibility and as sacred fidelity, had lost their force, and had been supplanted by a new set of conceptions, more practical perhaps, and more suited for the exigency of the times, but certainly of a lower grade of moral altitude.   Expediency had taken the place of duty, self-interest that of loyalty.   New nations had come into being full of these new ideas, made up of new men.   Commerce, manufactures, and art were growing, and with them a new class engrossed in them, and placing in them the highest good ; the mercantile spirit was crowding out the chivalric and religious ; actions were estimated by their profitableness rather than by their excellence.   The old restraints on the royal power were passing away in every land of Europe ; great kings had grown up who plunged their people into the horrors of dynastic wars, and were supported by the new classes that were rising into power through their wealth, and who saw in the widening range of national existence wider opportunities for their trade and speculation. It is true that the material comfort of the well-to-do had wonderfully advanced ; the world was richer, busier, working more hours a day and more days in the week, but the division of the product was becoming more and more uneven. The old insecurity of the middle ages, when robber barons plundered the merchant trains along the high roads or harried the cattle of the neighboring barony, had indeed been removed ; kings and merchants had joined hand in hand to put down this disorder and had succeeded ; but in place of the oppression of the weak by the strong had come the no less cruel plundering of the poor by the rich.

The substitution of wages for the older servile labor was not entirely the benefit it seemed. The serf who rose in the struggle for existence and became an employer himself, benefited by the change ; but the peasant

laborer who lost the security that his servile
tenure had given him, and became merely a
"hired servant," had little cause for gratitude. Large culture was superseding small ;
in some parts sheep-raising was supplanting
agriculture, throwing men out of employ-
ment and land out of cultivation, cheapening
the clothing of the rich, increasing the profits
of the manufacturer and the merchant, but
raising the price of food. Even soldiers now
fought for money and not for glory. The
days of chivalry were ended, the era of the
hired adventurer, the Landsknecht, the Free
Companion, had arrived, making war less
deadly indeed for the combatants, but fear-
fully fatal for the unfortunate countries
which were exposed to their brutality and
rapacity. But along with this there was a
brighter side. With this growth of material
wealth and development had come the arts
of leisure and refinement. Others beside
the monks now had time for study and re-
flection. Europe became self-conscious, and
with the recognition of self came the corresponding recognition of the external world.

Inventions followed one another with a distracting rapidity ; learning was encouraged, and a new world of thought opened out to the minds of men, at the same time and in the same manner as the new world beyond the ocean opened out its mysterious charms to the daring voyagers who had sought it. The age was one of unrest and of change. A new Europe had come into existence, and was trying to reconcile itself with its surroundings. Its movements were tentative, experimental. It felt about like a child which tries to grasp all objects that attract it, without regarding whether they are within reach or not. It is a period of vast interest, as it shows us a plastic civilization which had not as yet set into permanent and durable form. The force that moulded this mass into the definite shapes we see to-day was the great religious revolution of the sixteenth century which we know as the Protestant Reformation.

With this splendid, brilliant new life of Europe, as capable of development but as undeveloped as that of a child, the papal

Church had little sympathy. Its theory was fixed, its rules were established. It did not recognize progress, advance, or development. Its theologians had codified, systematized, and arranged all knowledge, divine and human, to their own satisfaction, and they did not like to see their work undone by the new learning that had come into the world in spite of their efforts. Their canonists had drawn up a body of laws to suit the conditions of mediæval Europe, and they were not inclined to recognize that Europe had ceased to be mediæval and had become modern. The Church's system had been organized for converting the heathen and teaching the ignorant ; but now the heathen were in the Church and not outside of it, the ignorant were the teachers and not the taught. To the modern age, as it was developing before its eyes, the papal system uttered its fatal " *non possumus*," which too often repeated brought on the revolution.

It was the papal system that stopped the way of all reform. Had it not been for this, it is conceivable that the efforts of those men

of the new learning and new thought, who **were** religious as well as enlightened, might **have** been successful in effecting a peaceful reformation; but against the power of resistance which it possessed, the efforts of Savonarola, of Colet, and of Erasmus were futile. Abuses were maintained because they were profitable; the papal supremacy was insisted upon, even after it had sunk to be merely the weapon of the prince of whom the Pope happened to be most afraid; and of the time when once rebellion began, and men saw that rebellion was possible, Europe was convulsed with the sudden uprising of men who would endure tyranny and abuses no longer.

We are told by one of the old ecclesiastical historians that, in Alexandria at the time of the conversion of the empire, there was a famous image of the great god Serapis, of great antiquity and honor, revered by the heathen, dreaded even by the Christians who could not free themselves from the superstitions of their infancy. Its removal was ordered by the authorities, but none dared lay sacrilegious hands upon it, until at last a Roman soldier, more pious or more sceptical than the rest, struck it with his axe. It fell, and out of it rushed a swarm of rats and vermin whose movements had made the mysterious sounds which the crowd had deemed the warning murmurs of the god. All respect then was lost ; the people rushed in with a shout, destroyed the idol, and cleansed the temple. So, until Luther was bold enough to strike his blow at the Papacy, none had dared to touch it. When this had once been done, men saw that the act was easy, and the religious revolution began which convulsed Europe for over an hundred years and has left western Christendom divided and weakened by its division.

It is impossible not to admire and sympathize with such men as Colet, More, and Erasmus, who sought for peaceful reform and fancied that it could be obtained. They were more amiable and attractive characters than Luther or Calvin or the later English reformers, but their idea was utopian. It was only possible if men could have been swayed by reason and not by passion, or if all men could have had their purity of ideal and singleness of purpose. The condition of the modern Roman Church shows us that it is possible to sweep away gross abuses and scandals, while retaining the Papacy. Whether it would have been possible to have secured also reform in doctrine and in discipline if no violent revolution had occurred, is an ineresting hypothetical question, but not one that is directly profitable.

The great causes which produced the Reformation were the growth of the new national spirit, which made men desire political independence and resent the domination of the Pope ; the growth of the new learning, which made them desire intellectual independence and cast aside the fetters of scholasticism ; and the growth of personal religion, which made them desire spiritual independence and repudiate the idea of priestly mediation. In the face of these, the Roman Church attempted to hold rigidly to the usurped dominion of the Pope and court of Rome ; to the abuse of authority

11

by the clergy and the scholastic theologians; and to the corruptions in doctrine and in practice; thus antagonizing the three strongest forces of the new life of Europe.

For a time it seemed as if the forces of conservatism would prove too strong for the spirit of reform. The princes preferred intriguing with the Pope against each other, to supporting national movements against the time-hallowed system of ecclesiastical unity. Their selfish aims and desires were satisfied so long as they could obtain their points and throw the suffering upon their people. Few of them were imbued with the spirit of nationality, or understood what it was that made their position so strong. If reformation had had to wait for the princes to lead it, it would have been long delayed. Again, the new mental life was assuming in a great degree a sceptical and irreligious character. It mocked at the miracles of the monks and ridiculed the syllogisms of the scholastics, but put nothing better in their place. The Humanists, as the men of the new learning were called, cared little for

Christianity. They were content to let abuses continue, so long as they were undisturbed by them. There was great danger that the result of the new learning, if it continued in their hands, would be the weakening of all religious sanctions. They ridiculed the superstitions of the clergy and the unlearned, and were teaching men that all Christianity was a delusion. Such a movement as this was powerful to destroy, but was not powerful to rebuild. The third reforming cause, the growth of personal religion, was the strongest, the purest, and the truest, and gave the impulse to the great revolution. Closely connected with the new learning and with the enthusiasm of national patriotism, it was able to blend both with itself in a threefold force, opposing the threefold tyranny that oppressed the world. Personal religion, sincere and true devotion to the service of God, had never been lost to the world, even in the darkest ages. There were always those who, in the midst of superstition and error, were preserved by their simple faith in God and their love and gratitude to the Lord who had bought them. There was never a time when the abuses were not felt to be abuses by a minority, a faithful "remnant," as an Isaiah would have called them, "the Israel of God," to use St. Paul's adaptation of the prophetic phrase. These were the men who had saved the religious life of Europe from extinction, men who were seldom in high place or position, but who, when they were, used that power and position manfully to resist the growing evil. Never, however, had their cause appeared less hopeful than in the beginning of the sixteenth century. The vested interests of the monks and higher clergy seemed to oppose a fatal barrier to all progress. Yet they had persevered, and had made use of the new learning to enable themselves and their followers to understand the Scriptures and the works of those early fathers of the Church who had written before the Papacy had arisen. The New Testament was re-translated ; the Vulgate was revised ; the original Greek of the sacred books was edited and printed and furnished with commentary and paraphrase.

Their efforts were hailed with joy by men who were like-minded, and welcomed even by the more sceptical Humanists, as weapons against the superstition and wilful ignorance of the rulers in the Church ; and thus they performed the most useful service of stopping the secularization of thought and of consecrating the new learning to the service of Christianity. But against them was ranged the conservatism of many religious men who were unwilling or unable to sacrifice familiar conceptions, and the self-interest of the worldly who saw their profits in danger if the simpler views and more spiritual conceptions should win the victory.

These latter opposed all reform, setting themselves firmly against any and all change, "loving darkness rather than light because their deeds were evil."

It is hard for us at the present day to realize the extent of the ecclesiastical tyranny that then existed, or the abominable character of the abuses that prevailed. The Church in the West was a great united empire of which the Pope was the head. Europe was divided into ecclesiastical provinces, each province into dioceses, and each diocese into parishes. Thus a graduated hierarchy was formed, closely connected together by bonds of discipline and self-interest, from the lowest priest in the village church up to the Pope on his throne in the Vatican. This ecclesiastical empire struggled hard to keep itself free of the civil power, and to maintain its own courts for the trial of offences concerning the clergy, with final appeal to Rome. The independence of the metropolitans in the various nations was kept in check by the presence of papal legates with plenary power, who, in spite of the resistance of secular princes from time to time, and in spite of secular legislation, grew more and more powerful, subverting the ancient authority of the episcopate and teaching men to look to Rome as the centre of all ecclesiastical power. Besides this hierarchy of the officials of parish and diocese, the whole of Europe swarmed with monks and friars who were devoted to the papal interest from which they had derived their peculiar privileges. For their services to the Papacy, and as a means of holding the secular clergy in check, they had been indulged with every kind of liberty, had been freed from episcopal oversight, and made of much more importance than those who were more immediately engaged in the work of ministering at the Church's altars. Originally professing poverty, they had amassed wealth to an unlimited extent, and had laid field to field until they had become lords of at least a third of the soil of Europe. Professing chastity, their monasteries had sunk to be little better than brothels where every kind of vice and luxury was practiced shamelessly. And it was such men as these that controlled and ordered the lives of their fellow-men from the cradle to the grave. Every action of a man's life came under their jurisdiction; education, religious privileges, marriage, sickness, death, burial, the testamentary disposition of property—all were in their hands, and all were used as a means of extorting money. Fees were charged for every act performed; and by playing upon the credulity of the

simple, and by harassing the death-beds of
the wealthy by the terrors of futurity, de-
luding the sufferers by their pretended power
over the pains of purgatory, they gained a
rich harvest and laid the whole Christian
world under contribution.   Thus the Church
was far richer than any of the monarchs;
but still the clergy were insatiable; from
small and great, from begging friar to car-
dinal, the cry was still, "Give, give," and the
court of Rome continued to make and au-
thorize fresh demands with an inexhaustible
voracity.   Such plundering would have been
a serious matter, even if the money had been
wisely spent; but men saw with disgust that,
instead of being used in advancing the Kingdom of Christ, it was squandered recklessly,
in wasteful and destructive wars or in
shameful and profligate luxury.   The wonder is, not that the more enlightened part of
Europe rose in revolt, but that the revolt
was so long delayed.

Yet it was but natural that men should
hesitate long before they struck a blow at
what represented the authority of religion.

The abuses were no new things ; they were the growth of centuries, and the theory of the papal dominion had become so ingrained in the religious conception of western Christendom that any rebellion against it as a system seemed indeed to be fighting against God. The penalties for heresy were frightful in their vindictiveness, and might well have deterred all but those who had the spirit of martyrs, and for men of tender conscience worse than the fear of the stake was the fear of hell. But the evil system had strained men's endurance to the uttermost. It had refused peaceful reform, it had closed its eyes and stopped its ears and hardened its heart, until it was too late, and the long-deferred explosion came at last, lighting a fire of religious hatred which raged for over a century and the embers of which even now have not done smouldering.

The explosion came in Germany, from one of those monasteries which had been the outworks of the papal line of defence. Martin Luther, a man of the people, a devoted lover of his country's independence, a trained scholar in the new learning, and an earnest and deeply religious man, protested against an atrociously coarse and blasphemous attempt to extort money from the faithful in return for pardons and dispensa- A. D. tions. The papal court, in indig- 1517. nation at the presumption of this unknown monk, attempted the usual measures of repression. Luther repaid threat by defiance, violence by violence, and soon was in open revolt against the Pope's authority. Germany was thrown into a blaze, and neither Pope nor emperor was able to silence the bold preacher or to prevent the spread of his ideas. When once authority had been defied, and defied with impunity, thousands were ready to espouse the reformer's cause. Little by little, the revolution spread into neighboring lands, while rapacious princes and nobles made it an excuse for seizing on the wealth of the churches and monasteries, and the cause of religious liberty was sorely hampered and discredited by the mixed multitude which hung upon the skirts of the movement. Every disorderly element

seemed to wish to ally itself to the Reformation; and it was only by the greatest tact
and skill that the German reformers were
able to steer their course prudently and to
rebuild as well as to cast down, to construct
a new system as well as destroy the old.

From Germany the reformation spread
north into Scandinavia, and westward into
Switzerland and France; and over all Europe
men's minds were in a state of wild excitement
at the changes which followed with alarming
rapidity. England for some time was un-
affected by the revolution. It was at this
period the most priest-ridden of all the lands
of Europe, and yet, at the same time, there
was no country, except Italy, where the new
learning had made greater progress. Its
monasteries were the richest in Europe, and
its prelates had been men of mark and moderation, many of whom, though they condemned the violence and the rebellion of
Luther were hoping for a peaceful reform.
The king himself was no mean theologian,
and was thoroughly in sympathy with Erasmus and Colet in their desire to sweep away

the abuses that had been allowed to grow over the practices of religion.

For twelve years after the outbreak of Luther, England remained strongly upon the side of the Pope, and then a personal quarrel of the king with the court of Rome was the occasion of a conflict with the Papacy, which resulted in the English Reformation. The Great Parliament was summoned, and it struck at once at the many abuses of the ecclesiastical system under which the laity had been groaning for A. D. years. The prelates were frightened into submission, and soon the rest of Europe saw with awe a country which still professed itself Catholic and still condemned the heresy of Luther, throwing off entirely the yoke of the Papacy and assuming the position of an independent national church. Rebellion against the nation's will was dealt with with stern severity; even the saintly More and the courageous Bishop Fisher were brought to the block for opposing the onward movement of king and people. The monks ventured to set themselves against the will of the liberated nation and its haughty monarch; and they were swept away ruthlessly, and their wealth thrown into the coffers of the State.

In Germany personal religion and patriotism had inspired the revolt. In England a movement at first political, was made use of to bring about religious reform; the men who removed abuses and declared their independence of the Pope had been inspired by a zeal for the Church and State of England, but they were not reformers in doctrine, and while Henry lived little change was allowed from the old forms of faith and worship. Yet, little by little, the reformers' doctrines were spreading even in England. One could not defy the Pope without coming at last to distrust the doctrines that the Pope maintained; and the zeal for political independence led soon to a zeal for spiritual independence. The great doctrine of the Reformation was that of the individual responsibility of each man to his Maker, a truth which had been obscured by the usurped authority of the popes, and by the system and teaching of the Mediæval Church. It came with the force of a revelation, and when once it had burned its way into a man's soul it became his controlling principle. It made him a free man, free from the dictation of priest and confessor, free from the fear of purgatory, free from the tyranny of a constant espionage upon thought and word and action, free from the bondage of ordinances that had weighed down the soul.

With the death of Henry VIII. the power A. D. 1547. fell into the hands of nobles who were inclined to the cause of the Reformation, and almost at once the new doctrines as they were called were recognized and made the law of the land. The Prayer Book was compiled and published, and its use imposed by law. The triumphant reformers abolished the mass, swept images from the churches, and thought, as Henry had thought before them, that they could impose a religion upon the people by force. They had no such claim upon the loyalty of the people as the king had had ; for, with all his tyranny and lust, Henry had been a loyal and patriotic Englishman, and had been loved and respected by his people. Their measures were disliked, their compulsion resented. The majority of the people preferred the old state of things as in the reign of Henry, and wished to preserve the Catholic religion without the Pope.

When the young king was hurried to his premature death, the revulsion that took place seated Mary firmly on the throne, and enabled her not only to restore the mass as it had been in her father's time, but to reconcile England with the Pope. Had she rested there, England might A. D. 1553–1558. have been retained by the Papacy and the course of the Reformation greatly changed ; but, with a suicidal conscientiousness, Mary felt herself obliged to punish those who had been the leaders of the Reformation in Edward's reign, as well as those who obstinately refused to conform to the Church as by law re-established. Her persecution, if we compare it with that which took place in France and the Netherlands, or even in Spain, was moderate. The total number

of victims was less than three hundred in all.
But the popular indignation was so great, the
hatred of persecution undertaken in obedience
to the will of a foreign power was so strong,
that the fires of Smithfield and of Oxford
severed England forever from the Papacy.
The martyrs went to their death with
heroic constancy, even Cranmer, who had
temporized in the hope of saving his life,
redeeming his character by the steadiness
and calmness of his behavior at the stake.
"Be of good comfort, Master Ridley," were
the words of the aged Latimer as the fag-
gots were kindled about them in the Can-
ditch at Oxford. "Play the man : we shall
this day light such a candle, by God's grace,
in England, as I trust shall never be put
out."

There is a sublimity in the constancy and
resolution of the early martyrs of the period
of the Reformation that, in some respects, is
greater even than that of those who con-
tended for their faith against the heathen in
the early days of Christianity. In the one
case the choice had been clear and distinct

between Christ and the pagan deities ; none could yield without apostatizing from Christianity. The decision which Cranmer and Ridley were called upon to make was between different forms of Christianity, and they might well have been pardoned if they had not felt it was their duty to die in defence of opinions that were believed to oppose the faith which was then, and for generations had been commonly accepted in western Christendom. But with the deep conviction that no voice of the majority could allow them to be false to the testimony of their minds and consciences, illuminated by the word and spirit of God, they "played the man" and, as the servants of God have done in every age, "they humbled their souls unto death, and were numbered with the transgressors," and the next generation testified to the work that they had done.

The religious wars which had been threatening ever since the beginning of the Reformation, now broke out in Germany and deluged the land with blood. The Gospel,

12

as in the days of old, brought with it not peace but a sword. In Switzerland canton strove with canton ; in France persecution at once repressed and stimulated the reforming movement. In Mary's reign the centre of the Reformation was at Geneva, where Calvin, an exiled French divine, ruled over his theocratic republic with a rod of iron, enunciating his grim Protestant scholasticism, devising and putting into practice a system of church government which should be independent of the State and powerful enough to serve as a form of organization for those who had thrown off the old forms of Catholic discipline. Beyond all others, Calvin's was the constructive mind of the Reformation. Luther had swept away the old system, but had relied too much upon the State to win a true independence for his reformed communion. In England the State had hampered and interfered from the first. It is true that to the State the inception of the movement was due, but from that time on its influence had been only to harm. In Henry's reign the cause of the Reformation had been soiled with the lustfulness of the king and the rapaciousness of his courtiers. In Edward's reign the bishops had been degraded into little better than state officials and England had been disgusted with the secularization of religion. In Mary's reign the powers of the State had suppressed the faith and burned the faithful. But in the ideal of Calvin, there rose a Christian body free from all state control, purely religious in its ends and aims, ready to direct and guide the State, but itself a pure theocracy. Not even the Church of Rome in her proudest day put forth stronger claims to ecclesiastical independence and the ecclesiastical power that independence involves, than did this passionless theorist, sharply, keenly logical, merciless in his conclusions. His republicanism was a necessary corrective to the too great tendency to lean upon an arm of flesh, which prevailed elsewhere in the reforming countries.

In theology also Calvin was constructive. He was the first great Protestant scholar and theologian, a Scripture critic inferior only to Erasmus, with a trained scholastic mind, able to formulate Christian doctrine in the light of the Reformation, in a manner worthy of one of the mediæval masters. He thus rendered Christendom a doubtful service. He furnished an organization strong enough to enable the unchurched reformers to face the organization of their enemies; he gave to Protestantism a body of positive doctrine about which to rally, making it a positive faith rather than a protest against abuses or a plea for reform; but in so doing he laid the religious thought of the new movement under the bondage of a stricter and more logical scholasticism than that against which the early reformers had protested. The Reformation till then had been a plea for free-thought. Where Calvinism was accepted, the human soul was again brought into subjection. But it furnished a magnificent fighting discipline and a fighting faith, and more perhaps than any other one cause prevented the reconciliation of Protestant countries with the Church of Rome. It has leavened all the churches, even those which have not accepted its theories of church government, and the spread of its doctrines and methods in France, Germany, England, Scotland, and America is a testimony to its strength. It did a great work in organizing Protestant thought for the great struggle which was yet to come with the Papacy. Its weakness lay in its neglect or rejection of much that was precious in the traditions and discipline of the past, in its failure to appreciate the value of historical continuity, and in its fatalistic theology, which, while a form of faith for heroes and martyrs, inspiring men to fearless daring and to tireless effort, was capable of being misused in a way that was subversive of morality. Few greater men have ever lived than Calvin, if we measure greatness by the influence which he has exercised. It is, however, an open question whether his influence should be reckoned as beneficial.

Mary of England died in 1558, broken-hearted at the failure of her life, having lost the hope of children, lost the affection of her husband, lost the love of her people, and lost

even the approval of the Pope. With ring-
ing of bells and shouts of rejoicing her sister
Elizabeth was welcomed to the
throne. The daughter of Anne
Boleyn could hardly be a Romanist ; the
daughter of Henry VIII. might be trusted
to have force and decisions of character
enough to make her wishes known and
her will respected.

A. D.
1558–1603.

There was little doubt of the result of her
succession to the throne, and soon the work
of Mary's reign was undone and the kingdom brought back to the reformed faith.
The chief opposition to the change was from
the prelates, but they were silenced and deposed ; a new hierarchy, still connected by
its orders with the past, but made up of men
of the new learning and the newly-revived
ancient faith, took their places ; and the
Church of England assumed the position and
character which it has preserved ever since.
The lawlessness that had characterized the
reforming movement in Edward's reign was
repressed. New spirit was put into the old
organization, and the people of England,

with the exception of a small minority, were glad to accept the wise and judicious compromise that preserved to them the dignity and authority of the ancient church while giving them the liberty of the reformed religion.

The weak point in the Church of England lay in its connection with the State. Its bishops were secular officials, and mingled ecclesiastical and secular power in a way that did not benefit the State and that caused the name of bishop to be abhorred by a growing portion of the population. This defect led in the next century to civil war, to the temporary overthrow and spoliation of the Church, and to the separation from its communion of many devout and earnest men who had been trained in the school of Calvin.

But the first result of the Elizabethan reformation was religious peace and the growth in piety and devotion that peace will bring. Her accession occurred at a time when the condition of Europe was most critical. Defeated and discouraged, Charles the emperor had resigned his crown and had

betaken himself to the monastery of Yuste,
and France and Spain had once more been
involved in war. Hardly had Elizabeth
ascended the throne when a chance thrust in
a tournament killed the king of France, and
placed upon the throne a boy who was married to her most dreaded rival, Mary of Scotland, and who was moreover under the influence of the most bigoted of the Roman
Catholics. The wars in Germany had ceased,
but the wars in France were about to begin
and to vex that land for over thirty years.
In the Netherlands the immortal contest
was just beginning between Romanism and
foreign oppression on the one side and Protestantism and national independence on the
other. Europe was fast dividing itself into
hostile camps, and the Pope was, like his predecessors of old, preaching a crusade against
those who ventured to dispute his will.

For a time England was dealt with ten-
derly, in the hope that a reconciliation might
be effected, but in 1570 the patience of the
Pope was exhausted, and the bull of excom-
munication was issued which declared Eliza-

beth deposed and her removal a righteous act. From this time on, it was war to the knife between the Protestants and the Catholics. Yet, from one cause and another, the final struggle was delayed for eighteen years, until England had grown strong and rich and united, until a new generation had grown up who knew popery mainly by tradition or by its evil fruits which were visible in the world. When the blow fell England was ready for it, and the Invincible Armada, as the Spanish fleet was proudly called, was boldly met and encountered. A storm, which swept the great galleons helplessly to the far north of Scotland, completed the discomfiture which the English gunners had begun, and the shattered fleet struggled lamely home with only a third of its original strength. " *Flavit Jehovah et dissipati sunt,*" was the inscription Elizabeth ordered upon the medal that was struck in memory of the deliverance ; "This is the Lord's doing and it is marvellous in our eyes." With the defeat of the Armada the conflict was ended for England. Never again was the Church in danger of forcible measures from the Roman party. In France the long and cruel religious wars were also approaching their end, and in the Netherlands the valor and constancy of the Reformers had won victory and independence. But in Germany long years of struggle were yet to pass in which men should murder one another in the name of religion, and it was only when the country was exhausted with warfare and bloodshed that peace was finally made in the Treaty of Westphalia in 1648.

Meanwhile the Church of Rome itself had undergone many changes, and had, in a sense, been also reformed. The first rapid victories of Protestantism had come from the earnest faith of the early reformers assaulting the countless abuses of the mediæval system. As long as Rome was merely on the defensive, merely concerned in maintaining the past, careless of the iniquities which that past enshrined, so long its defeat was sure and the new life had an easy conquest. But when the spirit of devotion and personal religion was revived in the ancient Church;

when it swept away the worst abuses, and set itself to win converts by persuasion rather than by repression ; then it recovered its strength, and was able to bring back many who were tired of the divisions of Protestantism and repelled by the severity of Protestant theology and practice. It should not be forgotten that Rome had her share of truth, that her cause was strong with the attractiveness of her grand historic system, with her claims of unity, and with the burning love and enthusiasm of the new Roman missionaries who now rose up to do battle for their Church's cause.

It was a very different thing to contend with the obscurantist monks, who loved their abuses and worshipped their superstitions, than for the men of the second generation to hold their own with the eager Jesuits, who longed to be martyrs and who brought into the controversy minds carefully trained in all the learning of their times and hearts full of love for the Roman Church and of zeal for the promulgation of its doctrine. The Papacy in the end of the sixteenth century was far different from what it had been at the beginning. It was no longer with careless voluptuaries or with worldly warriors that the Protestant churches had to deal, but with men of deeply religious character, hard, cruel, bigoted, it is true, but men with a definite purpose and a clear conception of the ends they wished to attain.

The Council of Trent had been a failure as far as promoting peace and unity was concerned, but it had done for the Roman Catholics what Calvinism had done for the Protestants ; it had given them a definite creed and a distinct theology. It was the fatal answer to the violence of Protestantism, and has made reunion an impossibility so long as its decrees prevail. All the energies of the Papacy were now bent upon recovering the ground that had been lost, and with so much success that they were able to confine Protestantism within much narrower limits than it had once possessed, and to reconquer much territory that once had seemed to be devoted to the Reformation. This would have been impossible for the men of the

age of Leo X., and was only accomplished
by the improvement which the Reformation
had wrought even among those who most
bitterly opposed it.

The influence of the Papacy was established
by the Reformation in the countries that adhered to its obedience. It had been dropping
into a decaying senescence when it was
aroused by the great convulsion. Never
again did the Pope recover the position held
by the great popes of the middle ages, as far
as domination over secular affairs was concerned ; but as the ecclesiastical head of the
Roman Catholic church he receives to-day
greater homage, and his influence is far
greater, than in the old days before the
Reformation.

The surest sign of reviving life and energy
is in the zeal of spreading the Gospel ; and
when Protestants rested, weary from their
conflicts and exertion, the Roman church
took up the work. Devoted missionaries
journeyed all over the world and preached
the word of life to the heathen. India, China,
Japan, Africa, Paraguay, and the forests of

Canada, all resounded with the grand war cry of the Jesuit, "*Ad majorem Dei gloriam*." When at last these too seemed to weary and to be corrupted with worldly aims, then Protestant England in its turn woke up to its missionary duty and sent its representatives with a simpler faith and at least an equal self-devotion.

In Europe during the latter half of the seventeenth century and the first half of the eighteenth, a lassitude seemed to fall upon religious enterprise. Each party was engaged in holding the ground that it possessed, and preparing itself in quiet and repose for fresh endeavors. The Church of England had had a stern discipline in the revolt of the Puritan party from its obedience. Its unhappy connection with the State hampered it in its relations with its own members, and it was compelled to see some of its most earnest and devout children driven into separation and schism by the mistakes of those who ordered and regulated its action. The Protestants in France were either suppressed by force or driven into exile, and ceased to form an element in the religious life of the country. In Germany men were weary with strife and only too thankful to be allowed to rest and recuperate. But the spirit of the Gospel was not dead, and, though too often in contention and strife, Christ was preached, the sacraments administered, and men taught to look forward from the evils of this present life to the glory that shall be revealed.

The present century has been the most remarkable of the four that have passed since the Renaissance, both for the remarkable development of the intellectual and material energies of Europe and the new Europe in America, and also for a corresponding awakening and quickening of the religious life. The great convulsion of the French Revolution in the close of the last century, "dissolved compounds," to use Bacon's phrase, broke up the old conditions of affairs, and stimulated the world to fresh activity in a way only to be paralleled by the earlier religious revolution. Religion, which seemed somnolent in the eighteenth century, has aroused itself to a vigorous and active life. No longer content with the promise of that only which is to come, it strives to realize the profit of godliness in this present world, entering into its life, concerning itself with social problems, recognizing perhaps more fully than in any other age its mission to preach the gospel of present comfort and deliverance to man. Its missionaries have crossed sea and land, and are found in the remotest corners of the globe, Romanist and Protestant rivalling one another in their zeal in seeking out the lost and bringing them to the knowledge of Christ's redemption. Charitable organizations at home, the care of the poor, the sick, the dying, the abolition of slavery in Christian lands, the general elevation of the moral standard in every land, testify to the wonderful activity which has characterized the Church of the West in these recent years. God has not suffered man's mistakes and follies to destroy his work; rather, we may reverently say, He has made use of these very mistakes and follies to extend His Kingdom.

After the fearful contest of the religious

wars the Church of Europe had seemed exhausted, willing to accept its religious divisions, satisfied if it was able to maintain its ground against the growing scepticism of the times. It has now recovered its activity, its zeal, its love of the souls of men, its spirit of progress; may we not hope that, as this blessed life develops more and more in the souls of its members, they will come to realize "what dangers they are in by their unhappy divisions," that missionary rivalry will give way to missionary unity, and that thus, little by little, the old divisions may be healed, and all Christians may be once more joined together in the bond of peace?

We have become unfortunately so accustomed to the divisions of Christendom that, in the quiet and ordinary work of the Church, they fail to impress themselves upon us as they should; we take them for granted as part of the existing order of the world; but when the earnest workers of the rival faiths meet, in their holy work, in the slums of our great cities or in the plains and marshes of the distant heathen lands, religious division

13

assumes a different form, and men learn to
see how hateful it is, how it hinders the
Church's work, and causes the enemies of
God to blaspheme. From earnest missionary
activity, from love of the souls of men for
Christ's sake, the blessed unity will surely
come.

And we of the Anglican Communion may
hope that, as our own Church was led by
God's providence to take a middle position
between the opposing extremes at the time
of the Reformation, it may serve as a point
of union where men of opposing schools may
come together hereafter. Preserving as
we do the historic organization and the
continuity with the past, and yet, maintaining that no church, or priesthood, or
sacrament can take the place of the direct
relation between God and each individual
soul ; we may hold out our hands to
welcome into Christian fellowship both Romanist and Protestant. Our liberal and
broad theology, which shrinks from defining
too closely the unspeakable mysteries of God,
has room for Roman, Lutheran, Zwinglian,

Calvinist, so long as they leave their anathemas behind them and bring with them only their benedictions. God grant at least that no action on our part may seem to hinder or delay this blessed possibility.

What then, may we ask, has the Reformation accomplished ? To answer that question one only needs to compare the Christian Church in the west to-day, with what it was before the Reformation. The contrast between Leo X. and Leo XIII. is no more striking than is the contrast between the Roman Church of 1500 and the Roman Church to-day, reformed from the worst of its superstitions, and overcoming the evil effects of those that remain by the earnestness of its faith and the depth of its love for the souls of men. Compare the Church of England to-day with the Church that is revealed to us in the reports of the Great Parliament in 1529, with the Church of Edward's reign and its rough iconoclasm, or with that of Elizabeth's reign and its subservient bishops ; see the work that it, and its children of the dissenting bodies, are now

doing in the world, the zeal for God, the
enthusiasm for righteousness and mercy.

Much indeed remains yet to be accomplished ; but no man can fairly read the history of the last four hundred years without
being impressed by the marvellous progress
which the Christian Church has made in that
time.   There are no four centuries in history,
except those first great centuries that saw its
growth from the hundred and twenty to a
multitude which no man could number, that
are so rich in the triumphs of grace as are
those which have elapsed since the Reformation.

Thus we may see how, throughout the
many ages of its history, the Church of Christ
has advanced, according to the law of the
life which was implanted in it in the beginning.   Like the mustard seed, it has grown
from the smallest beginnings to mighty
strength by the development of the principle
of life which was contained in the germ ; like
the leaven which the woman took and hid
in the meal, its increase has been in accordance with the wonderful property by which

even the lowest forms of life are enabled to continue and perpetuate their existence. Changed though its form may be, varied as are the features of its outward appearance, it is still the same organism, the same Body, as it was in the upper room at the first Pentecost, one and the same through all the long centuries.

In different ages it has had different forms of work to do, and different rates of progress. Considered alone, special periods may seem retrograde ; but when we view them in the light of historical development we may read the story of advance, even in the times of bitterest struggle, and may look hopefully forward to the victories for the cause of Christ which the next age shall surely see, and confidently onward still to the time, of which the eye of faith may even now catch the first glimmerings, when the kingdom of this world shall become the kingdom of our God and of His Christ, and He shall reign for ever and ever.

THE END.